To my grandparents, Emma Lou and Don.

The Skinned Bird
Essays

Chelsea Biondolillo

KERNPUNKT • PRESS

Cover Art: Chelsea Biondolillo
Book Design: Jesi Buell

1st Printing: 2019

ISBN-13 978-1-7323251-1-1

Diagrams of United States, Creative Commons CC0, and Thundercloud, World Book Encyclopedia. Zugunruhe figures/captions are from Emlen, "Migratory Orientation in the Indigo Bungting, Passerina cyanea. Part II: Mechanism of Celestial Orientation" (1967).
All photographs © Chelsea Biondolillo, 2018

KERNPUNKT Press
Hamilton, New York 13346

www.kernpunktpress.com

Table of Contents

I cannot write about beauty, which rankles and drives no
chariot of fire before me, but instead lies out on a slab of
wood in the rain, and stays neither wet nor dry
Bianca Stone

I'm not
allowed to be alone with scissors.
I will always find a way to dig.
Aimee Nezhukumatathil

I am repurposing the animal. I will do it gently, carefully. I will
do it with love.
Kristen Arnett

PART I: CRITICAL LEARNING PERIOD

CRITICAL LEARNING PERIOD

Song birds, or oscine Passeriformes, with fixed song repertoires learn to sing in four steps. The steps are studied, in part, because many linguists believe that these same four steps describe human language acquisition.

The first step in song acquisition is called the critical learning period. This is when chicks begin to recognize their parents' voices along with neighbors of the same species, and they differentiate between those voices and other sounds.

*

My parents were married for three years before I was born, and they lived together for almost three years after. The shape and sound of their love is unknown to me. I have no idea how he courted her or when the courting became something else. I do not remember the words they spoke to each other in the days and months while I lay in my crib, listening.

I know what my mother said to me and what I said back. These are stories I've heard often. Before I could talk, I had night terrors, she tells me. I would scream inconsolably in my sleep. The pediatrician said this was normal for some babies.

She tells me about the day I choked on bottle milk while lying in my crib, and how the sound of it sent her running to me; how afterwards, I would choke and gag whenever I wanted her to pick me up. It was a sound she could never ignore, she says, eyes squinted theatrically at the memory of my manipulation.

I would stand in my crib and yell (so early! so advanced!) MOM. MOM. MOM. MOM. And then one day, after a moment, DARLENE. I wonder, now, if I sounded like my father when I said it.

SILENT STAGE

A chick in the silent stage of development might make alarm sounds or cry for food, but it does not sing. This period can last up to eight months. A number of ornithological research studies document that a range of memorization and comprehension activities are occurring during this stage.

*

I would've been memorizing and comprehending while my parents' relationship collapsed. I have only two vivid memories from that time, and both are soundless. One is of watching Sesame Street while my mother did '70s-style calisthenics in front of the couch, next to me. The other is of my father throwing clothes out of a dresser drawer. For years, this memory seemed to be of a comic gesture, something he might have done to make me laugh. My point of view was low-angled, as though I were standing in the doorway to their room, which is long in my mind's eye with dreamlike perspective, like a hallway, at the far end of which was their bed. The memory itself is just a flash, no more than a six-second clip of motion: arms, clothes arcing up and over. Years later, after my mother told me about the night we left, the nights leading up to our leaving, I realized that he was not performing for me. He was tearing their shared bedroom apart looking for evidence, for proof.

*

Studies on white-crowned sparrow song learning pre-date the studies of Stephen Krashen, a linguistics and education scholar, whose input hypothesis describes how secondary languages are acquired in human speakers. Krashen never mentioned birds, but his own work underscores the importance of the silent period. He believed that comprehension naturally led to communication. Though some of Krashen's arguments are thoughtfully criticized now, they influenced language learning programs for decades, and continue to do so.

*

Over good wine and a perfectly grilled steak, my latest lover tells me all of the things his ex-girlfriend didn't like, wouldn't do, failed to appreciate. Each exasperation has a moral; it's a little lesson I'm to learn. He calls this sharing himself, and I hear myself repeat back to him, *Yes. Please. Thank you.*

*

Before I was born, my mother sold light bulbs door-to-door while my father was at work. This made it difficult for him to monitor her, so he pressured her to go back to restaurant work.

At the restaurant, he could drop in from time to time. He could check to make sure she wasn't flirting any more than was necessary to get her tips. When she told me about the light bulb job, I was in grade school and using her old sample case to cart around my art supplies. It had a socket housing at one end. She must have been able to screw a bulb into it for demonstration purposes. When she told me about having to go back to the restaurant, I was an adult. By then, I was familiar with what it felt like to be monitored by my lover.

*

Both humans and songbirds learn their complex vocalizations early in life, exhibiting a strong dependence on hearing the adults they will imitate, as well as themselves as they practice, and a waning of this dependence as they mature.

— "Birdsong and Human Speech," Doupe & Kuhl, *Annual Review of Neuroscience*, 1999

*

Recent work with zebra finches shows that certain neural gates open or close when young birds are learning songs from their male tutors. As fathers sing new pieces of song, 'learning' neurons fire, but pieces of song that the chicks have already learned do not have the same effect. In fact, when they hear a song repeated, an inhibitory response is triggered in their brains. The researchers track these responses using implanted electrodes weighing less than a penny and "freely flying" finches.

One of the researchers says of their findings, "We see that the brain changes how it listens to the father once it's learned part of that song." She finds that sweet.

*

I don't remember my first breakdown, because I have cried a lot for as long as I can remember. I cry when I'm tired, when I'm frustrated, hurt, sad, scared, whenever I am overwhelmed. But at some point, during my last year living at home, and my third year in college, I tried to talk to my mother about it.

I had been afraid to tell my mother that the crying worried me, that it sometimes seemed a thing out of my control, like a car still rolling forward though my foot was mashed into the breaks. My skin felt hot and my stomach churned when I imagined the words I would have to say. Words like hysterical, and maybe even crazy. I have been afraid of other conversations in my life; it always feels like this. This time, I was most afraid that she would just say to try harder and I couldn't imagine how to do that.

Instead, she said, "Maybe you were awake the night we left. I thought you were asleep, but maybe you were awake."

*

When I'm alone in the house, and my lover is far away on one of his frequent business trips, I sit down on the area rug I bought—to protect his Peruvian mahogany floors from the sharp edges of my second hand coffee table—and attempt to call up the loudest sobs I can. *No one can hear you*, I tell myself, *Now is the time to get it all out.* I think about his small cruelties, his reminders, admonishments, the long months of summer stretching before me. But I almost never make a sound.

SUBSONG

During the next phase of their learning, baby birds practice the sounds of their song without actually communicating information. The subsong has been likened to "babbling" and has also been called a period of "vocal play." I learn in an ornithology textbook that individuality is important to birds, too. They transform and improvise from the collection of themes and syllables that were memorized in stage one.

During a lecture on birdsong acquisition, a professor of mine mentioned that birds deafened prior to or during the subsong period would never be able to effectively reproduce a song recognizable to other birds.

I'd been interested in birdsong for years before this class. I could distinguish the raspy song of red-wing blackbirds from the other feeder visitors at a very early age. I was able to mimic towhees, jays, robins, and finches by grade school. But this idea of birds being "deafened" was new. It was a word that required investigation. A glance at the methodology sections of several papers found mention of lesions, implants, and pharmacological interventions. During studies like these, birds are induced to sing in a variety of ways: the removal of their mate or parent, recordings of known or unknown individual birds playing nearby, and by electric stimulation via implanted surgical steel electrodes. Researchers who use these methods are supposed to follow humane procedures so as to minimize animal pain, suffering, and distress.

*

He was drunk at the time, she said, and in the throes of one of his paranoid fantasies about infidelity. He raged. He had a gun, and later, a knife. He was threatening to hurt her, and himself. When he finally passed out, she bundled me up. We left. I don't remember any of this, and can't imagine it, because I can't picture my father doing any of these things. He has never had a drink of alcohol in my presence. She said so little against him when I was young and she never denied his rare weekend visitation requests. Though I can't imagine it, I know it's true. Something in my quickening pulse must remember it, even if I can't call the memory up.

In high school, snooping around an old file cabinet of my mother's, I found a poem written in his handwriting. It was melancholy and dramatic and not very good. The only words I remember are "tears" and "gray." I don't know if he wrote it *to* her or *for* her or if he just wrote it and it was stuck in between other papers that she needed to keep. I stuffed it back where I found it and mentioned nothing for over twenty years.

As soon as I told her that I'd once found such a poem, she said she probably still had it somewhere. "You know how I keep things," she added.

*

My mother tells me my father had no patience for fussing. If we were at someone's house and I began crying or whining, "like a baby," she explains, like I was supposed to, she means, we'd have to leave.

I tell her, perplexed, but not with any disbelief, that I have seen very little of this side of his anger.

"I guess I inspired it in him," she says, in my voice.

Yes. Please. Thank you.

I assure her that I've heard similar sentiments from his ex-wives and their children. "If you did, it wasn't personal," I say.

*

"But most of the finer detail of the song is learnt by the young bird when, in its first breeding season, it first comes to sing in competition with neighbouring territory holders. There is little doubt that this is the way in which local song-dialects are built up and perpetuated. Full [songbird] song is thus an integration of inborn and learned song patterns, the former constituting the basis for the latter."

—"The Learning of Song Patterns by Birds," W. H. Thorpe, *Ibis*, 2008

*

My mother would sew my dolls dresses from fabric scraps and once, she converted a particle board bookcase into a four-story Barbie dream house with some leftover carpet corners and contact paper. Many of my own first art supplies came from her stash.

She also taught me to succeed. I stayed up all night to finish projects on time. I worked two jobs to save enough money for my first year of college. After my own marriage ended, I took every promotion I could get until I had a down payment for a house. If you do what needs to be done, things will always work out: this is my mother's song.

But in looking up the gruesome details of songbird experiments, I find this: songs are learned from conversations just as much as from tutors. I know so little about the conversations that I heard first. I worry often about the things I learned to say in my father's voice. About my own predilections toward any voice that sounds like his.

But too, about the sound my voice still makes crying out in defiance of his demands, even though I have disavowed his demands for decades.

SONG CRYSTALLIZATION

The final step is to turn the babbled song into an adult song.

It can happen within weeks of the young bird's first attempts, or it can take months, depending on the species. The bird picks a few sounds from his practice and then organizes them into phrases and perfects their timing, such that he can communicate with others of the same species.

*

When I try to ask my mother about our time in my father's house, she chooses words carefully. "It is extremely difficult to live under the scrutiny of a jealous person."

I explain the critical learning period, about wanting to know more about the first words I heard. I do not say that I am waiting for someone to come home, that when he does, I will talk to him in a voice I don't recognize. I'm afraid that she might tell me to stop trying, to get as far away as I can. I will, and soon, but today I can't yet imagine how to do that.

"You would've heard some very ugly things. Some very... ugly things." I can hear her mind stumbling and skipping, with regret perhaps, or possibly, sudden insight. My skin gets warm and I don't want to hang up the phone with this widening space between us.

Sometimes knowledge is a burden you can carry for someone else. I want to take this knowing from her and pack it back up.

I tell her that even scientific analogies have their limits. I tell her starlings and mockingbirds continue to learn songs throughout adulthood. I tell her about the zebra finches, how they learn to ignore the sound of their fathers' voices.

"That's reassuring," she says.

I pace in front of the large picture windows with a dust mop in my hands and the phone in the crook of my shoulder. The windows let in so much sunlight. I imagined it would be good light to work by—the way it glows on his fine wood floors like a magazine ad for floor wax. But it only does that when the wood is spotless, I've learned. And keeping it spotless takes a lot of work. Outside, a juniper titmouse, then a junco, then a rock dove, stop by the porch in search of food. One by one, they find none.

"Plus, we aren't birds," I say.

"That's true. We aren't."

I shake the dust mop out over the trash and move to the broom. We start talking about birthdays. Mine is coming up and there are so many after that, in August. Among them, my father's, which neither of us mentions, among them, my lover's. I've been knitting him a pair of socks. He'll only put them on once, when I ask to see if they fit. I'll take them with me when I leave.

SAFARI CLUB

We ask for menus. In the background, knives and forks clatter against simple white plates. Over my grandfather's shoulder, a leopard is frozen in mid-leap, his chipped claws sink into a gazelle. The gazelle has been painted with red stripes to heighten the illusion of split-second predation.

I always ask to walk the perimeter of the restaurant after we've placed our orders. My grandmother takes my hand and we head first through the Arctic, where ermines, captured behind glass, are stuck forever half-white. The walrus head is impossibly large. She hoists me up so I can rub my fingers across his hard muzzle, play the whiskers like strings on a ukulele. Then we waltz under the jaguars, wired into once-sleek arcs over the dance floor. The killing isn't worrisome— the blood is paint, the postures of fear and survival, posed. The hunter and taxidermist are long dead, too.

Back in the Serengeti, the food has arrived. A lion carries an antelope in his mouth while a hyena menaces from across the glass case behind my chair. Dik-diks and warthogs edge the display, watch the drama unfold. The lion is dusty, and there is a cobweb between the dangling antelope legs.

My grandfather saws through his Swiss steak while my grandmother navigates her Monte Cristo into and out of her raspberry jam. She dabs a red spot on her blouse with a corner of napkin that's been dipped in ice water. I always get the fisherman's platter and devour everything but the oysters. We eat, arms languid and unhurried, while hundreds of dull eyes look on.

KICK BALL CHANGE

It was country-late: the air outside getting cool and damp and purple. I sat at my mother's parent's dining table making clothespin dolls while the crickets whined and Teddy-dog sat by the back door smacking his muzzle at errant flies. The doll project made me feel like Laura Ingalls Wilder. I clipped red and white checks and velvet strips from grandma's quilting stash. My fingers, the wood, the table, were shiny with glue. All of my girl-clothespins had straight hair, because I could not get the curls to stay on. I wanted my grandma to draw the faces, because she could draw tiny swoops that turned into eyelashes and lips, but she'd gone to her room and closed the door. She did that sometimes, for hours, days. But I always had something to keep me busy. If I ran out of clothespins, there were jars to fill with grasshoppers.

Suddenly, the bedroom door flung open, and my

grandmother sashayed down the hall in red velour sweat pants and shiny heels.

"I bet you don't know how to tap dance, do you?" she said, her grin wide and electric. She grabbed my hand and pulled me into the tiny, dingy kitchen with the pink walls and cobwebs. "You'll learn tonight! Let's start with a kick-ball-chain. Don't you have any clackety shoes? We'll make do. We can make do." She started to hum some tune, and I tried to follow her steps, shuffling on the linoleum, our fingers laced, stuck knuckle to knuckle.

ZUGUNRUHE (MIGRATION) I

Portland, OR (1973-1995)

Phoenix, AZ (1995-1996, 2009-2011, 2015-2017)

New Orleans, LA (1996-1999)

Santa Fe, NM (1999-2000)

Austin, TX (2000-2004, 2006-2009)

Rockville, MD (2004-2006)

Laramie, WY (2011-2013, 2014)

Ucross, WY (2014)

Hamilton, NY (2014-2015)

Hastings, NY (2015)

Estacada, OR (2017-

PART II: SILENT STAGE

HOW TO SKIN A BIRD

Your first and only incision will be right over the sternum. All birds have a bald patch there. Blow lightly on the breast until the feathers begin to part and you can see the pale skin beneath.

Rest your finger there for a moment. Feel the bone your blade will follow. Make a wish, if you must, and then slice from collar to belly carefully.

I used to keep the letters my father had written to me in a box with all of my other letters. There were three of them, all written before I was eight, on lined paper with a ripped, spiral fringe. He put them into the envelopes he sent my mother. Otherwise, they were empty, except for a check, always made out for $75. Sometimes the envelopes came from Alaska or Tahiti.

When I was a little older, if I saw the mail before my mother, I would feel the envelopes, to see if they were thicker than just-a-check.

*

You will need to cut the spinal column and trachea before you go any further. To do this, carefully work a small surgical probe between the skin and neck muscles at the very top of your cut. The curved tip is blunt, and if you advance it slowly, it shouldn't tear the skin. Work it behind the neck until you can see it on the other side. Then slide the lower blade of a scissor along the steel. When you can see the scissor's point, cut.

On larger birds, you may need to cut two or three times, blindly. This is why the probe is important: it keeps you from cutting through the back of the neck and beheading your specimen.

I stayed at my father's parent's house a few times as a child, usually when he was visiting, too. Even though he had a local apartment twice, I never stayed at either one. In the second apartment—which he took me to once for just a moment—I had my own room. I looked in through the darkened doorway and saw a bed and bedside table, no lamp, and then we had to leave.

I never stayed alone with him until I was in college. This doesn't feel ominous, just disconnected.

His parents lived in a double wide trailer, in the yard of a landlord I never met. I slept in his little brother's old room.

*

After the neck is cut, you will slip the wings from their bones like a jacket.

To do this, repeat the following steps for each side: using your fingers, pinch the humerus below the shoulder joint and slide the skin away from the muscles like you are taking off tight jeans or pantyhose.

Keep rolling the skin from the structure until you feel a boniness branch off from the ulna, just past what would be the elbow joint. This is the first primary feather. Use your fingernail to scrape it out—as you would a wasp's stinger in your own arm. There will be a few primaries. Pop them from the bone one by one, and then cut the humerus close to the shoulder. Be careful not to cut through the skin. Both wings should be intact in the final specimen.

Uncle John had hundreds of comic books. I lay in that strange bed and read them through hours of sleeplessness. I preferred Casper and Archie to the superheroes because of the simplicity of their drawings. Hulk and Iron Man comics seemed busy and cramped; I couldn't always tell what was happening.

My grandmother, his mother, was an Avon lady; she sometimes let me take home tiny lipstick samples of last season's colors. She had an impressive collection of facsimile whiskey decanters shaped like famous people and a kangaroo skin my father had brought her from Australia.

My grandfather had a wooden leg and a glass eye. I was not told this, but discovered the prosthetics while snooping. I was told that he used to drink homemade corn liquor that he filtered through loaves of coarse wheat bread. He did this a long time before I was born. I don't remember who told me about it.

*

When both wings are free from the body, gently peel the back skin from the muscle. If it sticks, as can be the case with some freezer-burned birds, use the probe and scalpel to loosen or cut through the scab.

You will cut the legs by rolling the skin away from

them as you did with the wings, but stop sooner, before you get to the scaled leg skin. Cut the thigh bone even closer to the body than you did on the wings.

Now pinch the tail ligaments and cut just above where you can feel the feathers end. If you cut too high, it will be a bit messy, but not unsalvageable. If you cut too low, the tail will fall off. This can't be fixed, so err on the side of a mess.

My father's mother would fry trout in thick oil for dinner.

We ate peanut butter and mayonnaise on white bread for lunch. I asked that this sandwich be put in my bagged lunch, when I got back home to my mother.

For breakfast, my grandmother would make tiny pancakes for my father and me. He would put butter and jam on them, instead of syrup. He would roll them up like cigars and eat them with his hands. So would I.

*

The body, separated, should resemble a very small version of a fryer or turkey. Notice that the muscle tissue of songbirds, however, is all dark meat.

You will carefully collect tissue samples from the

breast, heart, and liver now, and determine the sex of the bird. You may also need to collect stomach contents.

Follow the photocopied instructions for this step. Use the small plastic vials, and consider all samples dry unless your collections manager tells you to store them wet, as is sometimes the case with rare specimens.

My mother never spoke ill of him; I want to say that. But the spaces between his contact swelled with meaning by the time I got to high school. First his father died, and then his mother. I asked him if I could come to her funeral, after I learned of it from my mother's mother—her neighbor. I smoked Marlboro Lights in front of him for the first time that weekend.

I stayed with him and one of the women he married a couple of times, once in Spokane and once in Pleasant Hill, California. She had older children, cut his meat for him, and talked in a nasal, baby voice.

He didn't travel overseas anymore but would frequently overspend. During one visit, he bought a new car and a giant television. Then, he got a nosebleed and sat in the center of his bed staring into space. His wife said, "Go comfort him!" Their marriage may have lasted ten years. Maybe less.

*

The head is difficult, so take your time.

Start by pinching the neck and working the skin away from and over the back of the skull. When you get to the eye sockets, use your scalpel to carefully cut through the thin membrane that connects the lids to the eyes.

You will need to keep the majority of the skull intact, to maintain a natural shape, but the soft tissue should all be removed: tongue, eyes, brain. Use caution so that when you cut out the tongue, you do not damage the hinges that connect the upper and lower maxilla.

The last time I stayed at my father's house, he was living alone in a near-bare apartment outside of Alameda, near a marina. We ate out, because the only thing in his refrigerator was a whole roasted chicken from the grocery store. He lamented my inability to cook. He showed me his cupped palm, full of old wedding bands. My mother's was not there, he said, as he clamped his hand closed and carried them back to wherever they'd been hidden. Did he think I might have asked for it? It broke, he said, making a joke of it.

I awoke the next morning in his (only) bed with his arm around me. I spent the rest of the week on the living room floor without comment.

*

The specimen will be used for study; it isn't intended to seem life-like—keep that in mind as you finish. After washing and drying the skin, you will use cotton wrapped around a small dowel to replace what you have extracted. Use enough cotton to create a sense of fullness, in the eye sockets, in the belly.

Tie the legs together, so they do not splay, and attach the specimen tag using a square knot. Paint the ends of the string with clear nail polish. Then close up the original incision.

After college, after my own failed marriage, he regained an interest in me. I tried to be polite when he came to visit me in Washington DC. I met him downtown, but did not invite him to my house.

A few years later, one of his girlfriends called me to say he was depressed and would I please call back later to cheer him up? He'd mentioned her once. She had a little boy, he'd said, whose name was spelled 'Jesus.'

"It's pronounced 'hey-Zeus'," he'd said.

I know, I thought.

He had told me her name, but I'd forgotten it and so

had hung up on her the first time she called, thinking it was a wrong number. She spoke very little English. The conversation was frustrating for us both. I didn't call back.

*

You may be tempted to take your needle and thread and sew dozens of the smallest stitches you can, as though attention to detail could hide the hole you've made. Resist this urge. Everyone expects a hole in an empty skin. Dip your needle once twice three times and then pull the thread tight. It's enough.

When I stopped answering his emails, he would telephone. The calls came every year or so, between girlfriends or wives. Once, late at night in a Barcelona train station, I was confused by the time difference and answered my cell phone, thinking there must be an emergency. He was bored and lonely. He made a joke about how long my master's degree was taking.

When I stopped answering the phone, he started to text. He always tells me first, that he's broke, and second, that he's single.

*

Before you position the bird to be dried, stick one straight pin through the base of the bill vertically from bridge to chin. Thread a small piece of twine through the nostrils and around the bill, using the pin as an anchor to cinch it tightly closed.

Use as many pins as you need to hold the specimen in exactly the position you want on the board. The head should be facing forward or slightly up, the wings tightly folded, right leg over left, and tail feathers spread just to the width of the body. With proper preparation, it will keep this shape through decades of routine handling.

THE STORY YOU NEVER TELL

I w   ut
I v   my
hus   r a
do   to
ser   e. I
wa

                                                     zz
lon   for
the

                                                     tic
bey   the
wo   all
ha   ere
sup   are
ou   we
left   led
us all into the room and we sat in a circle on plastic scoop-

shaped chairs and she handed us each a glossy, over-sized

pam

That   in

conv   d a

lot, e

"No   nt,"

the r   ort

limp   She

had   g to

make   to

you,'   g to

conr

       to,

and   by

religi   not

creat

       ned

enha   ned

that   the

deve   age

to describe other components of the cellular organization.

She was very careful to never say "it." She told us that

she   and

tha   her

har

           her

boc

           ing,

son   me

alre   was

at—   do

wha   ver

dec   We

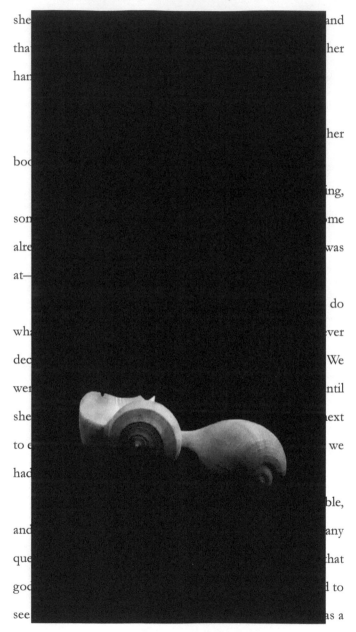

wei   ntil

she   ext

to e   we

had

           ble,

and   any

que   hat

goc   l to

see   s a

giant child in a man's body—bringing a third into our boozy

mix was in no one's best interests.

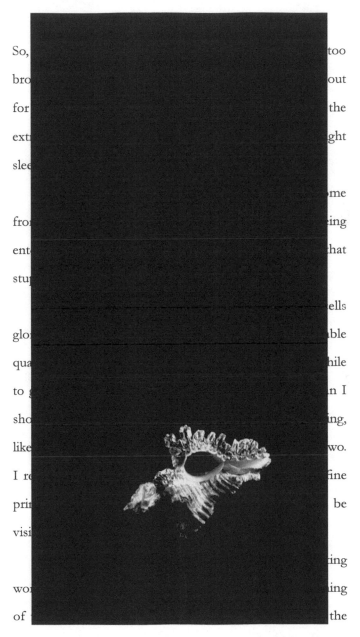

So,   too
bro   out
for   the
ext   ght
slee

                                                         me
fro   ing
ent   hat
stu

                                                         ells
glo   ble
qua   hile
to   n I
sho   ing,
like   wo.
I r   fine
pri   be
visi

                                                         ing
wo   ing
of   the

receptionist and said yes to her questions. Yes, this is what I want. Yes. But my buzz was gone. What I wanted now was for

the

I r   t. I

rem   hat

my   my

free   and

helc   "It

hur   uld

do   me,

whe   h I

cou

I n   we

wer   t've

bee   to

sus   and

no   ubt

awa

                                                          cal

pub   ded

spl   ng,

and the kind of song that locals and tourists alike loved like mad.

Sor

I w   hat
I u   ean.
Gil   nce
dov   ppy
cur   l in
witl   n a
plac

Wh   and
mil   and
Ma   ose
yea   hs,
and   hat
hap   or
twid   ring
wor   g

them off and fighting for their attention. I didn't know how to say no the right way. Or yes.

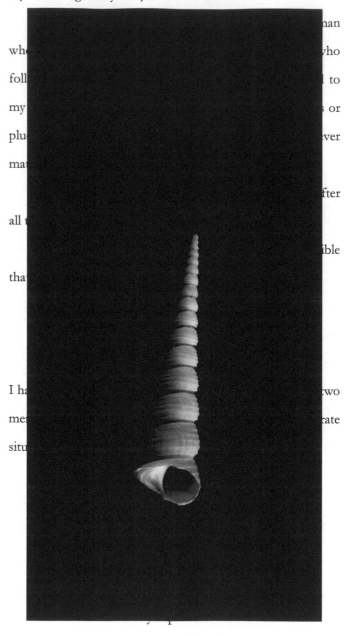

han
wh   who
foll   to
my   s or
plu   ver
mat

fter
all t

ible
that

I ha   two
mer   rate
situ

38

But to be fair, back then, that's not what they were. No one I

kne   lity

was   one

of   ons

and   Or:

trou   at's

and   off

whi   ent

the   nk?

An   but

thir   ore

like   let

you   es,

bec   It's

a st   s at

a st   ful.

I w   em.

But   that

swung around like a tether ball that I just kept pounding.

None of this has anything to do with Dr. John or New Orleans

or e   I'm

not   ing

I n   The

ven   list

of

Ard

                                                        up

and   no

whe   he

gra   my

mo   ay,"

and   on

mir

                                                        ctly

wh   She

ass   der

ma   nd.

Wh

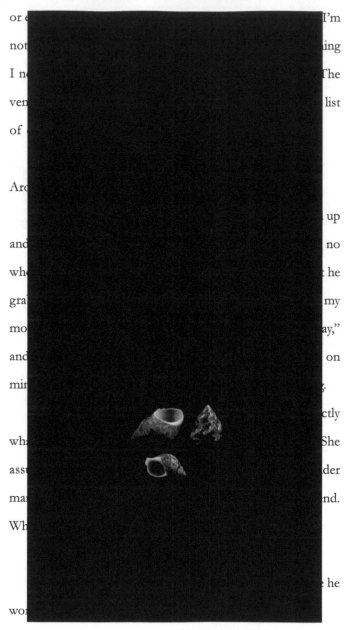

                                                        he

wo

Terrible things happen to terrible girls who get around make bad decisions. Either these things were terrible, and so was

I—   ed.

We   ver

kicl

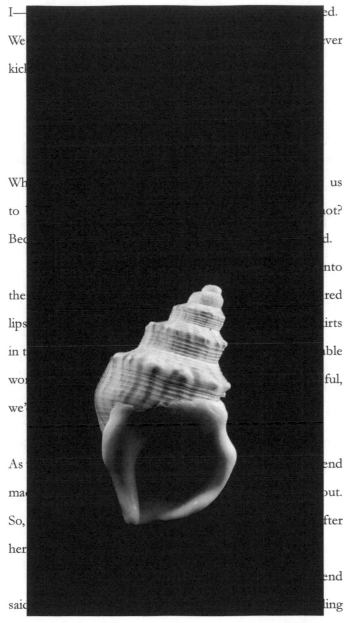

Wh   us

to   iot?

Bec   d.

                                                            nto

the   red

lips   irts

in t   ble

wo   ful,

we'

As   end

ma   out.

So,   fter

her

                                                            end

said   ing

in line at the grocery store, trying to get a good look at them out of the corner of my eye. I nodded silently at the checker

wh

We ons

wer hed

and ous

tha Just

me. uch

har eyes

clos uld

not ow

wh

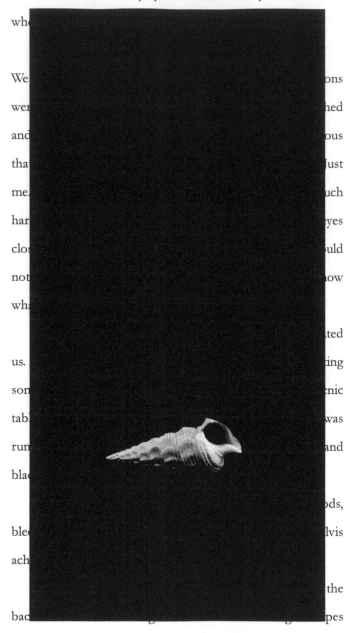

ted

us. ing

son nic

tab was

run and

bla

ds,

ble lvis

ach

the

bad pes

across her face, twisting her features until I thought that maybe girls could be monsters, too. We whispered behind them while

the   reet

cor

 so

gro

ve'd

stas   ing

of   She

said   fun,

for   ten

pie

On   irl's

hou

en,

whi   use

she   her

to l

nny

Bo

not

the   urn

bowl cut that looked perpetually mussed.

The first time I had seen him, he was looking over a

tall 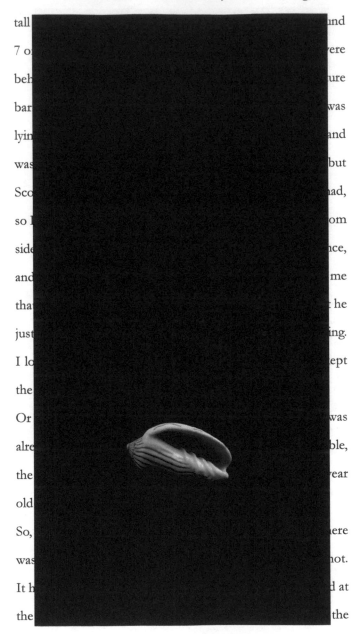 und

7 o   ere

beh   ure

bar   was

lyin   and

was   but

Sco   had,

so I   om

side   nce,

and   me

tha   t he

just   ing.

I lo   ept

the

Or   was

alre   ble,

the   rear

old

So,   ere

was   not.

It h   d at

the   the

things we had done in my mind, because I don't remember

saying no, even though I was terrified of anyone with white-
blo

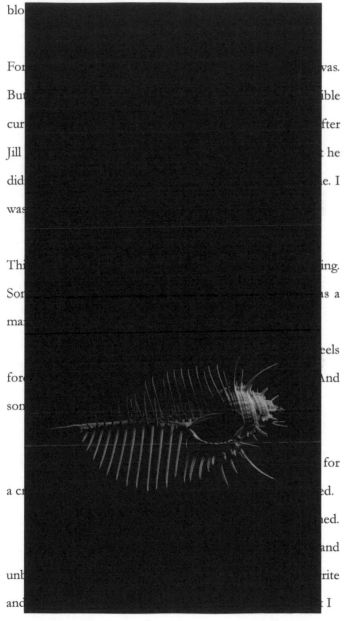

For   was.
But   ible
cur   fter
Jill   he
did   e. I
was

Thi   ing.
Sor   s a
ma:

                                                               eels
for   And
son

                                                               for
a cr   ed.
                                                               ed.
                                                               and
unb   rite
and   I

Either it's all terrible and I'm terrible, or, if I'm here and I'm happy, I have to find a way to be grateful for it all. Either

you   eat

tor   our

owi   ver

hav   we

for   wall

tha

                                                                       re's

got   d o

kay   just

a h   of

coo   too

mu

CRAZY

Kathleen had just pulled me out onto the porch, away from everyone else, away from Claire. Even though Kathleen is Claire's mother, Claire almost always calls her Kathleen, not Mom. Claire is my best friend. But her mom is weird.

If Kathleen was mad, she would've said so right in the kitchen with everyone else. But she saved her weird stuff for in private—unless it was totally public. Like, once, for Claire's birthday, she hired some random guy to come to school and sing her a song. We ran away from him for ages, but eventually another teacher found us and we had to go to Barb's homeroom class where of course a crowd had gathered, and this guy sang Claire a song about how beautiful she was and gave her balloons. Claire said she was so embarrassed—but no one else's mom ever sent in a guy to sing for their birthday. So I'm not so sure.

That year, Claire got a big mirror on a carved wooden stand for her birthday. Claire said Kathleen made a speech about Claire's womanhood and seeing her true self. Sometimes I think that mirror was a dumb present for a sixth grader.

Now, with Kathleen dragging me out on the porch, I was all tense. She made me look at her. I really wished she'd act like a regular mom and just leave me and Claire alone.

"I want you to know how special, and beautiful you are." *Oh my god.* "Now, look at me. Do you understand that you can do anything you want to? In the world?"

"Yes." My mother told me this all the time but more like, Quit screwing around, you're the smart one.

"And you are a beautiful, smart, capable woman. Do you understand that?"

Eye roll.

"You need to understand that you are a beautiful and smart and capable woman and you are going to do amazing things. I want you to tell me you understand me."

"I do." I didn't mean to whine, but I did a little. "Can I go back in?"

"Yes. You can." She smoothed my hair down on my head and sort of patted it. I could tell that I hadn't answered the way she wanted. Like I was supposed to say, *Oh wow, you're right, suddenly you made me look beautiful just by saying it.*

I have beautiful hair (when I brush it) and beautiful eyes (when I'm not giving a look). But I am not beautiful.

My grandmother has taken hundreds of pictures of me, usually for practice when she gets a new camera lens. She has told me a million times that I can have a pretty smile, if I don't show my teeth and don't curl my lip so it gets mashed under my nose. If I hold very still.

She says the problem is that I insist on doing unattractive things. Like popping my finger out of my mouth to make a water-dropping sound and slouching.

My mother has pictures of me that she says are very pretty. She says I'm photogenic. I guess that's a kind of beautiful.

But it's not the kind of beautiful that strangers see. They tell me that my hair cut is nice.

Grown ups act like Claire is stranger-beautiful. This one time, at a bus stop, this crazy guy was freaking out about how beautiful she was. He said, "If you were standing naked before some guy with your hair ass-length, you'd make his WORLD." He also said he wanted to craft Claire a *purse*. Out of *leather*.

He didn't say a single word to me the whole time, even though I was standing right next to her and no one else was around.

I don't get it because Claire wears the same size pants that I do, but everyone knows I'm fat. One time, I mentioned this, and Claire got mad at me and said that she wasn't the same size as me *at all*, that her waist was much smaller, only most jeans didn't fit her right. And then I said, "Do you mean you aren't fat, you just have a fat butt?"

I guess I have a fat stomach and she has a fat butt and that makes all the difference to hippie guys at bus stops. She also has blond hair and blue eyes and straight teeth whereas I have *dishwater* hair, and *hazel* eyes, and I am not supposed to show my teeth when I smile.

Claire doesn't tell me I'm beautiful, the way her mother does. I don't tell her she's beautiful either, since everyone else does. I remind her that her ass is gigantic whenever she says something about how another gross guy said something creepy to her.

One time I told her to stop bragging about all the gross guys and she told me it can't be bragging if she doesn't like it. I don't think that's true, but she tells me I don't understand, since creepy bus stop men leave me alone.

But that isn't true, either. Bus stop men don't leave me alone. They just don't say anything that I can tell like a funny story. They stand really close when I'm sitting on the bench and there's no where else to sit, so their cocks are right in my face. They sit next to me on the bus when I have a window seat and pretend to fall asleep so I have to push them when it's my stop.

Once a bum came into our school, because of the open campus. He followed me until I was stuck in a corner by the auditorium. Then he slapped his hands on the wall next to my face and leaned in like he was going to kiss me. I dropped to the ground and got away.

Afterwards, all the kids told Barb how he must have been crazy because he wanted to kiss me.

Can you imagine? How crazy he must've been?

ENSKYMENT

horned lark

The first shock was the lark's limpness: how its tiny head lolled in my palm unless cradled. A dead animal on the ground lies still, posed however it fell. The great murderer in my life, a striped cat, ran away to die by herself—I never had to wrap her soft body in a towel. And her trophy mice, tucked in my dresser drawers, were still stiff when my mother whisked them away to the trash.

I had internalized an assumption about the permanence of rigor mortis without ever testing it. Rigor passes.

In ornithology class, the hunters can already ID all the ducks and are never surprised at the specimens.

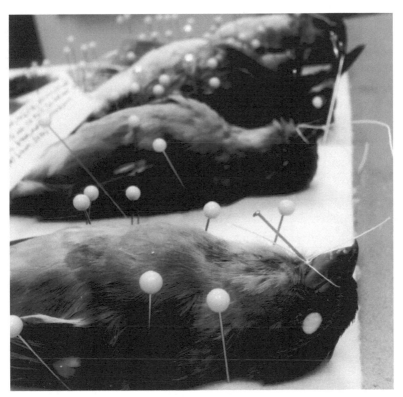

Figure 1

brown rat

We only lived in the little house for three years. I still slept in a crib and watched Sesame Street while my mother did calisthenics. I do not remember eating or sleeping there. I don't remember what the yard looked like. I do not remember my father's shape as he moved through the rooms, whether he yelled or swayed, but I remember turning my head to watch my mother, standing in the shape of a star. Her legs wide, she bent down to touch her right fingers to her left toes, then back up, then her left fingers to her right toes. And I remember turning back to Oscar the Grouch, and Grover, and Burt and Ernie. I don't remember Charlie, but I remember her telling me about him, often.

Charlie was a rat, and he lived in the basement of the little house. I never saw him, but my mother says he would scratch at the basement door whenever she was in the kitchen. She would open the door just a crack and drop a few pieces of dog food on the linoleum, she says. Charlie was our secret, because my father said absolutely no pets.

What I don't know: Where did my mother get the dog food? And, when we ran away from my father, from his vodka-fueled rage and his gun—who fed Charlie after that?

Figure 2

shore crab

Do you remember the first time you lied? The first time you held something small and hard and clawed to your belly, clasped inside a make-shift cage of mussel shell halves, even though you knew you weren't supposed to? Even though you were specifically told to leave it behind?

But once you'd held it, it became yours—to steward or ignore as you saw fit. It was delicious and terrible, this skittering responsibility, this sin.

Figure 3

the dogs

Our dogs don't die; like dissidents, they disappear.

Lobo was returned while I was at school, to a log-and-shingle house in the woods. My mother forgot to tell me, until I started to make up his bowl of dog food and leftovers that night. Pepper was stolen—by dog fighters, Tom muttered as though he knew it for a fact. Her jaw was wide and she was potato-tight with muscles, just what they wanted. Gus, a bright, but over-sensitive mutt, lived a long time at my grandparents' after we re-located to a new state. He must have died there among the blackberry vines and tansy.

But before them all: Baron. He was our first dog as a new family. We got him when their baby was on the way. My step-father named him after me (I saw once, on the registration papers), a long complicated name full of dashes, as my own had become. Baron was also taken—because of his pedigree, his show quality, Tom lamented, because of his beautiful lines. I remember this one photo: his daughter from before and I standing over Baron, competing smiles toward the picture-taker. I am happier, she seems to say. No, me, I counter. It is one of only two photographs of the both of us, the big sisters, and the only one I know of that dog. He never was fully house-broken and then he was gone. She moved away not long after the picture was taken.

In later family portraits, however, my mother, her husband, their daughter, and I smile as though we are something complete.

Figure 4

domestic cat

I told my mother what you did, and she said I can't come over anymore. She said you're running wild over here. She said you're too much for your crazy mom to handle on her own.

I can still see Smoky, the tomato trellis stuck to the side of your house, your black rubber boot with the red trim at the top, his long gray hair, his plastic flea collar, hooked. How he thrashed his head to the left and right, like a whip, trying to get free. How he froze after you kicked him. How he froze and never moved again, not even to go limp, like dead animals on TV do. And how you laughed at how dumb he was for not running away.

Figure 5

rainbow trout

My father took me fishing once when I was eight or nine. Already, I didn't know him, except as a rare visitor who drove me around on the motorcycle he kept at his parents' house, whenever he passed through town between jobs.

We fished at Eagle Creek. I don't remember if I had a pole or if my job was just to watch him catch something.

He jerked the first trout from the water and I saw him use a rough flick of his hand to pull out the hook. I put my hand to my mouth and pressed two fingers against the gum line of my top teeth. I focused on his hands, because his eyes were so unfamiliar.

He did not warn me before he slapped the fish hard against the rock between us. I flinched at the wet crack, and then I saw the fish go still. I knew nothing of fishing. I felt dizzy and afraid of him.

"It's to put it out of its misery," he said, flustered.

Figure 6

blackbird

I did not know the name *supracoracoideus* the first time I saw
the muscle. A great blue heron, standing in the stream as
I rounded a bend in the trail, leapt. I saw a great flexion
behind the wings pull back and strain, for a second, before
the bird sprang aloft: flight as effort.

Later, under the blade of the scalpel, under the skin of a
blackbird, it was a deep red. No different than any other
muscle.

Figure 7

box turtle

Long before my parents bought their house in Phoenix, a small turtle had wedged itself under the gray wooden floor of what my mother would call the "cabana" out by the kidney-shaped pool. She thought the cabana unsightly and unsafe. She asked Tom to tear the roof off and pull down the rickety supports and peel up the frame. When he did, the turtle was there, wedged tightly in the L of two 2 x 4s. It had been there awhile. It might have gotten stuck, or it might have crawled there to die. It was just bones and dark, damp meat by the time he found it.

Tom said, "Figured you'd want it."

I filled a bucket with bleach and dropped the whole thing in. I used a wooden spoon handle to break up the pieces. After a day, the shell began to peel, the color coming off in thin sheets like fingernails. I picked each bone from the pulpy water and laid it out by the pool to dry and whiten in the sun. Tom frowned at the bones from behind his newspaper.

I pressed my thumb against the point of its tiny beak and imagined how the skeleton would look on my bookshelf.

In less than an hour, a thunderstorm rushed over the house on its way to Mexico. The wind tore palm leaves off the trees and threw the remains of the cabana all over the yard. When it was over, I could only find the turtle shell and four leg bones in the bottom of the deep end.

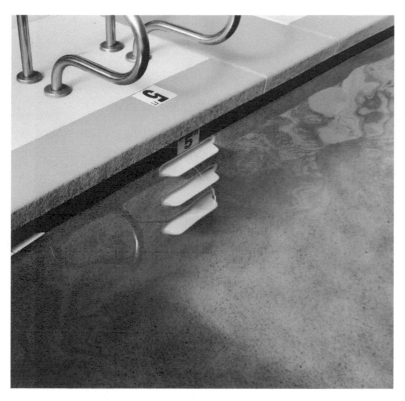

Figure 8

borer beetle

My future landlady knows I am newly separated from my
husband. She nods with an exaggerated sympathy when I tell
her I need to move in soon. I am to understand that she, too, is
without a husband—but she doesn't say whether a deliberate or
fateful act made her so.

She has deep creases in her cheeks and wears too much mascara.
My new apartment is in the *Casitas de los Cornell.* Her name is not
Cornell.

She lets herself into my apartment from time to time, to leave me
notes. She tells me the rent is late or that the electrician will be
by, on blue or pink post-it notes. If I still lived with my husband,
I might feel bolder. I might tell her she isn't to come in when I
am not at home. Instead, I think, there's nothing to hide here.

One day there is a margarine tub on my table. There is a pink
note on it that says, "I found this and thought of you and your
bugs." She means the dragonfly and green beetle I have under
glass by my bed. I imagine her leaning over the small table,
adjusting her readers to get a good look, her elbow by my pillow.

The margarine tub is opaque yellow with red writing. I have no
way of knowing what is in it, and whether whatever-it-is is alive
or dead. After a while I look anyway. A giant black beetle rattles
across the bottom of the tub. Something has crushed it, almost
in half; there are guts and legs all over. I put the lid back on and
leave the tub on the table where I found it, for several weeks.

Figure 9

house sparrow

He says you can't predict how tough a bird's skin is by its plumage—the most delicate looking birds are often the most rugged. He demonstrates how I need to use my thumbnail to scrape the wing feathers out of their tiny sockets in the ulna bone. My first specimen, a house sparrow, forgives my fumbling. My crooked stitches disappear under her resilient breast feathers.

When I was a waitress, I always looked for the small numbers stickered to table edges or on the wall, above the condiment caddies, at every other restaurant. The looking was involuntary: my attention had been shifted by habit.

Now, I see how one bird tips forward, swiveling on fused pelvic bones; how another ruffles, then smooths, its thick flank feathers.

Figure 10

wild geese

Just days after I moved in, you changed. Where once you had courted me, now you ranted. Your voice raised, you judged me and found me wanting.

On long walks down your country road, I found some peace in the quiet. All that summer, while I tried to make the best of us, I watched a goose raise a clutch of goslings. She started with seven, and while they were still gray puffs of down, she led them around the pond at the foot of the hill. One day, there were six and then, five. It is hard to know whether a bird is mourning. Across such a distance, she looked the same to me, as surely I did to her.

The five that remained grew bigger. I planned an escape, kept the details a secret. After their pinfeathers sprouted, they were four, and then three.

She must have watched those three closely. They grew leggy and tall as the summer wore on. Then the whole group would stand on the road as I walked by, no longer diving into the water. Still she stayed near them and hissed a warning as I passed.

At the end of summer, you borrowed a gun and shot both of your cats in the woods to show me just how much need offended you. I was sure that in time you'd kill me, too. I rented a truck for my things. You raged, shook your fists as I packed my boxes, told me I'd never have it this good again. I walked by the pond, to make some gesture of goodbye, but the geese were already gone.

Figure 11

PART III: SUBSONG

PHRENOLOGY // an attempt

In the beginning, science class was exhilarating. I had not yet learned to be squeamish like a girl, so I would pick up anything.

That delirious green beetle I found desiccated on the windowsill had a back so soft that my fingertip wasn't sensitive enough to appreciate it. I held it to my eyelid, finally my lips. I rubbed one spot, over and over, until the softness had left it.

I touched an electric fence once[1] when I was ten, at a friend's house. The voltage was low enough that it thrummed through me, like a sine wave from bones to tendons to veins.

> MY DEAREST ESTHER, - & ALL MY DEARS TO WHOM SHE COMMUNICATES THIS DOLEFUL DITTY, WILL REJOICE TO HEAR THAT THIS RESOLUTION ONCE TAKEN, WAS FIRMLY ADHERED TO, IN DEFIANCE OF A TERROR THAT SURPASSES ALL DESCRIPTION, & THE MOST TORTURING PAIN

I was not deterred at all, and thought often, later, of getting that feeling back: the hum of electrons coming together.

Later, at the beach, tiny jellyfish washed up in daunting numbers under windy skies, looking for all the world like egg whites, emptied of yolks. I wanted to hold one, but my grandmother said they had a sting like an electric shock. As soon as my grandmother turned her back, I reached out a tentative finger. The mass had a solid feel; it had an unexpected skin around the clear softness. There was no shock at all.

---

1   *A lot of words in English confuse the idea of life and electricity, like the word livewire.*
Laurie Anderson

Differentiation. Orogeny. Anion. Mitosis. Batholith. Telophase. Syngamy. Escape velocity.

Things separate from the whole: atoms, stars, continents, stones, leaves, cells, skin, parents. Things also come together.

It isn't a good idea to be the girl who likes torn skin and spiders and snakes. You might find yourself differentiating from the group. Stratifying[2]. If you are the girl who looks when a bug is stepped on or a mouse is half eaten by your own cat, your orbit may widen out and flatten, like a comet, your view moving farther from the center to an outer perimeter. It will feel as far away as Cassiopeia, as Arcturus[3].

WHEN THE DREADFUL STEEL WAS PLUNGED INTO THE BREAST - CUTTING THROUGH VEINS - ARTERIES - FLESH - NERVES - I NEEDED NO INJUNCTIONS NOT TO RESTRAIN MY CRIES. I BEGAN A SCREAM THAT LASTED UNINTERMITTINGLY DURING THE WHOLE TIME OF THE INCISION - & I ALMOST MARVEL THAT IT RINGS NOT IN MY EARS STILL!

Sometimes an obsession feels like looking out different windows and seeing the same landscape, like turning the radio dial and hearing the same song over and over.

Let's face it, no one ever believed I was going to be a scientist: I lacked focus and drive, but still my mother bought me the Gabriel Tri-Lab-Pak

---

2   *We shall of course be told that they must go into the water before they can learn to swim; but what is proposed is not to teach them to swim: it is to throw them all at once into a fathomless ocean, where they will drown themselves, and pull down those who were swimming there, or trying to swim before them.* Francis Parkman, "The Woman Question" 1872

3   *If you can't give me poetry, can't you give me poetical science?* Ada Byron, Countess of Lovelace

for Christmas, 1983. She would not allow any of the red-capped chemical bottles to be opened after reading the warnings on them. I cracked open the sulfur bottle, from time to time, having never smelled a rotten egg, but I left the rest closed. Instead, I dutifully performed identification streak tests on the non-volatile ceramic tile, and scratched pennies with the mineral specimens—to rate their hardness against the copper. The glossy silver hematite scratched a surprising rusty line; the quartz gouged the penny like a surprising root into the thin membrane of a shin. Suddenly the world seemed full of shifts, full of things that were more than they appeared to be, harder than they seemed.

WHEN THE WOUND WAS MADE, & THE INSTRUMENT WAS WITHDRAWN, THE PAIN SEEMED UNDIMINSHED, FOR THE AIR THAT SUDDENLY RUSHED INTO THOSE DELICATE PARTS FELT LIKE A MASS OF MINUTE BUT SHARP & FORKED PONIARDS THAT WERE TEARING THE EDGES OF THE WOUND - BUT WHEN AGAIN I FELT THE INSTRUMENT - DESCRIBING A CURVE - CUTTING AGAINST THE GRAIN, IF I MAY SO SAY,

The Tri-Lab-Pak came with a microscope. I peeled scabs off my knees and scales of dead skin from the bottom of my summer feet and examined the pieces in the light of the lens' mirror. A wart that fell off my left big toe looked just like regular skin, which was disappointing. I wanted to understand something larger from the seeing. Once, I cracked a plate from over-tightening the dial, trying to get closer, to get inside the cells.

He said you mustn't drop the tarantula, that if you did, its belly would burst open like a tiny watermelon. We all pictured the tragedy and gore of that undoing, then waited our turns. The man with the spider placed it carefully on my stiff, upturned palm. He was all nerves, explaining to the rest of the class the importance of moving slowly, of being serious, of being calm.

It felt ungentle, unlike a hamster or woolly bear caterpillar in every way. I concentrated on the rhythm of one leg—bristled like a pipe-cleaner then tapering to a point—lifting then stepping, as the weight of its fragile abdomen shifted with each step. I was too focused on not dropping it to be afraid.

WHILE THE FLESH RESISTED IN A MANNER SO FORCIBLE AS TO OPPOSE & TIRE THE HAND OF THE OPERATOR, WHO WAS FORCED TO CHANGE FROM THE RIGHT TO THE LEFT - THEN, INDEED, I THOUGHT I MUST HAVE EXPIRED

Later that year, someone came into the first-grade classroom and squeezed all of the monarch butterfly cocoons that were hanging in a row above the art table. It had to be an older kid, because we couldn't reach them. What came out of their onion-skinned green shells looked neither like what went in or what was supposed to emerge. They were still blended, a mix of land and air, when they were split open like grapes.

Most kids wouldn't hold the fire-belly salamanders after the herpetologist explained that their brightly colored skin contained poisonous alkaloids, which tasted bad to predators. All I saw was that hysterical orange stomach, and I greedily stretched out my cupped hands to take the squirming wetness.

I rested my thumb on its back, to still it in my hand; I watched its toothless mouth open and its lashless eyes blink. Later, in the darkened classroom, as the class watched a film on wetlands, I scratched deep grooves in my thighs. The hives were palm-shaped with raw finger-stripes, where my hands had rested as the film began. The best part, I remember, was how my hands didn't itch, only the skin they touched— like I was the poisonous one, now.

I am looking for a way to get at the experience of a thing, the memory of it, to better understand the meaning of it. I am expecting the process to be messy.

In the road once, in the fourth grade, after getting off the #10 city bus to Harold Street, I passed close by an opossum, torn open by tire treads. I knew it was an opossum, and not a cat, though much of its distinguishing characteristics had been ground into the pavement, because of its pink tail. Though I walked fast, and I knew it was wrong to look,[4] I still saw a movement among all the red and pale slicked shapes, between two ribs poking up. They were pink like her tail, and hairless, and they squirmed blindly: thirsty and shocked at the sudden cold.

---

4   *In an address to the American Society for the Prevention of Cruelty to Animals on Thursday afternoon, President John P. Haines made the following statment, referring to the killing of cats by teachers in the public schools for purposes of dissection:* "Women who practice it get fond of it, and women who get fond of cat killing are on the high road to homidcial mania... It has been asked why this tendency should be so stressed in reference to women. I reply that women are, to a large degree, the creatures of impulse." New York Herald, Feb. 17, 1900

I didn't want to do the catching or crushing or cutting, ever. Destruction was never the point. I wanted to see the aftermath; I wanted to know how things were unmade.

I spend an afternoon trying to find a woman pioneer in the field of electricity, but end up poring through reports of women who have been executed in the electric chair.[5] It often happens on accident like this, I don't go looking for the split open things or the dark insides. The first one was in 1899. By then, they'd figured out the voltage, and she went fairly quickly.

> *I ATTEMPTED NO MORE TO OPEN MY EYES, - THEY FELT AS IF HERMETICALLY SHUT, & SO FIRMLY CLOSED, THAT THE EYELIDS SEEMED INDENTED INTO THE CHEEKS.*

Could a phylogeny of the great and terrible things of this earth teach me anything about what captivates me? How can I create a taxonomy for all my dark fascinations?

In 1981, I was about to turn seven. My grandparents had taken me on a birthday trip to the beach almost two weeks early that year—no one remembers why. Maybe my mother and new stepfather had a trip planned for Memorial Day weekend; maybe my new baby half-sister

---

5   *My dear Mr. Governor: Please forgive me for bothering you ... I have been paralyzed for more than three years and I could not look after Gennie as I wants to. I know she done an awful wicked thing when she killed Miss Belote and I hear that people at the penitentiary wants to kill her. But I am praying night and day on my knees to God that he will soften your heart. If you only save my child who is so little, God will bless you forever.* Charlotte Christian in a letter to William Hodges Mann. Virginia Christian, age 17, was electrocuted on August 16, 1912

82

was sick. But on May 18th, a Sunday, I was in a small five and dime store on the Oregon Coast, worrying over a teddy bear. I was allowed to pick one as a birthday present, from what seemed like hundreds, each different from the others.

There was a very soft smallish bear that I liked a great deal, but it seemed silly to waste this amazing opportunity (ANY! BEAR! PICK! ANY!) on something so small. The biggest bear was not soft, but had matted dark brown fur, like a toy from a county fair. It had a yellow and black nose. It was almost as big as me. I picked this bear, the largest one, even though I remember very clearly liking the small one more. The remorse was already upon me

THE INSTRUMENT THIS SECOND TIME WITHDRAWN, I CONCLUDED THE OPERATION OVER - OH NO! PRESENTLY THE TERRIBLE CUTTING WAS RENEWED - & WORSE THAN EVER, TO SEPARATE THE BOTTOM, THE FOUNDATION OF THIS DREADFUL GLAND FROM THE PARTS TO WHICH IT ADHERED -

when we walked out into a rare sunny day and my grandmother pointed up at the sky, at the growing white cloud of a volcanic eruption.[6]

For days, back in town, I watched the cloud get taller. The Portland weather conspired, staying unusually clear of low, gray mist. The ash cloud looked white, though I knew from the television that it was towering over dark mud and seething pyroclastic flow. Dead trees,

---

6   *The eruption cloud is very solid-looking, like sculptured marble, a beautiful blue ... darkening towards the top—a wonderful color. One is aware of motion, but (being shaky, and looking through shaky binoculars) I don't actually see the carven-blue-sworl-shapes move ... It is enormous. Forty-five miles away. It is so much bigger than the mountain itself. It is silent, from this distance ... It looks not like anything earthy, from the earth, but it does not look like anything atmospheric, a natural cloud, either ... the shapes are far more delicate, complex, and immense than stormcloud shapes, and it has this solid look; a weightiness, like the capital of some unimaginable column—which in a way indeed it is, the pillar of fire being underground ... To us it is cataclysm and destruction and deformity.* Ursula LeGuin describing the 1981 eruption of Mt. St. Helens in her journal

dead deer, dead scientists, walls and roofs and stones, were all rushing over the banks of the Toutle River under that ghostly white shape. I nearly went blind from staring at it, trying to catch it moving. But it always looked perfectly still.

While watching the Brakhage film, *The Act of Seeing with One's Own Eyes*, I made the following notes:

Technicians silently split bodies open. One attends the cadaver of a young woman. Her breasts are still soft and full; they move, as they would if she were dancing. He cuts and lifts her skin from her ribcage; he pulls with firm movements, deliberate. The scalpel saws gently and she is opened like a suitcase.

AGAIN ALL DESCRIPTION WOULD BE BAFFLED - YET AGAIN ALL WAS NOT OVER, - DR. LARRY RESTED BUT HIS OWN HAND, & - OH HEAVEN! - I THINK FELT THE KNIFE TACKLING AGAINST THE BREAST BONE - SCRAPING IT! - THIS PERFORMED WHILE I YET REMAINED IN UTTERLY SPEECHLESS TORTURE, I HEARD THE VOICE OF MR. LARRY, - (ALL OTHERS GUARDED A DEAD SILENCE) IN A TONE NEARLY TRAGIC,

And I think of Fanny Burney, who felt this same motion. Fanny, who watched as seven men in black invaded her study with no warning. They had doctor's bags and her husband's permission. Fanny, who lay there under a handkerchief with nothing but a bit of laudanum in her tea, as they sawed off her breast. When they looked down through her skin and muscle, did they imagine they could see her heart behind its bone bars? They held her down. But, she says, she never fought them.

The body, for she cannot have a name any longer, is hollowed out, small wet sac by sac. Her gut, her heart, her lungs—all that propelled her —is weighed and bagged. An assistant, whose face we never see, washes her shell carefully. They move her body, and it looks easy; she's light now. Brakhage wants me to see how we can be unburdened; how, then we can be lifted as easily as an empty purse.

Her skin seems so pale and smooth, but I will never know if she was pretty: her scalp remains folded over her eyes and nose like a blindfold.

It takes several tries for me to watch the whole film through.

DESIRE EVERYONE PRESENT TO PRONOUNCE IF ANYTHING MORE REMAINED TO BE DONE; THE GENERAL VOICE WAS YES, - BUT THE FINGER OF MR. DUBOIS - WHICH I LITERALLY FELT ELEVATED OVER THE WOUND, THOUGH I SAW NOTHING, & THOUGH HE TOUCHED NOTHING

I wanted to try everything. After Mr. Hamilton's 8th grade biology class dissected cuttlefish, he fried one on a steel plate over a Bunsen burner. I was walking by and a girl dared me to try some. She was being cruel, but I didn't realize that until later. The rubbery texture resisted my teeth; there was no flavor beyond the pickling solution.

On some lunch breaks I would visit the chemistry classroom and watch Brutus, the school's moderately socialized python, eat a white rat. Chemistry got him because Mr. Hamilton preferred the docility of fish. On other days, I would ask to hold Brutus, but this opportunity was rare. I loved the paper-dry skin and cool weight of the snake across my shoulders. It pressed, encircled, all one tugging muscle. It was comforting, being held by the snake.

It was probably while wading in the river chasing crawdads that I saw a movement near a tiny pile of twigs and rocks. I lifted the sticks out of the water, but saw nothing, no scale, no antennae or eye. I placed them back in the water and waited until the caddis fly larva stuck two tentative legs out of its assembled shell. I picked it back up, and left it on a smooth river rock to dry. I wanted to watch it crawl back

SO INDESCRIBABLY SENSITIVE WAS THE SPOT - POINTED TO SOME FURTHER REQUISITION - & AGAIN BEGAN THE SCRAPING!

into the water, watch that process of return – as though I were young Darwin with a Galapagos lizard, but instead of hucking it into the sea, I was dragging it out. The larva did not show itself. It did not save itself. Instead, it retreated further into its shell, trying to escape the air that evaporated all movement out of its skin.

There was never any indication, outside of the cluttered confines of my desk top, that a girl could be a scientist. Or that my interests were even scientific. There was no proof that discovery could be a graceful, shining thing.

I learned later, through rumors and shouts and long silent looks not to mention waveforms or snakes or jellyfish. I dropped the microscope in a box and forced myself to stop announcing the names of birds on the long school bus ride home. I noted the way my classmates sat around me and smiled out at the world like open dandelions or full moons. I practiced that.

Years later, when the art college accepted my application, I was relieved to learn that very little science was required. That which intrigued me became too obvious with scalpel and lens at hand. Instead, I drew. My fingernails pressed half-moons into the blue wood of my pencils with a drive to get through the paper, under its skin. I carved deep grooves in linoleum and plaster blocks. I fought every surface, then smoothed wax, glue, and ink over the cuts I'd made. My drawings were of

- AND AFTER THIS, DR. MOREAU THOUGHT HE DISCERNED A PECCANT ATOM - AND STILL, & STILL, MR. DUBOIS DEMANDED ATOM AFTER ATOM.

dead grasshoppers, broken toys gone filthy with age, bones, bare roots growing over black, slick rocks: a topographical map to dark cracks in the ground, openings, still and quiet things, that which had been left over and behind.

In the studio I would tell myself, *there's nothing wrong with that.* But I had turned timid and over-careful. A fear had grown inside me where once there had been only fascination. There was no knife, no charged wire loop that could remove it.

I remember reading in a book in college, whose name I have forgotten, about a terrible operation. It was my ex-husband's book: he was very interested in Roman warriors and in Genghis Khan crossing the great swamps of middle Russia. But once I flipped through and found a short letter from a woman who had had breast cancer. She could feel the knife as it bumped across her ribs. She used the word *scraping*. She could hear and feel it scraping. That was over 18 years ago, and I still can't forget her.

It isn't until Internet keywords that I find her again. *scalpel ribs mastectomy historical eyewitness* Her name was Fanny. She lived for 29 years after the operation. How she must have been grateful for science, and terrified of it, too. How its song and its scream must have rung in her ears.

NOTES ON ARRIVAL, MAY 1994

Traveling through the desert southwest makes me write bad poetry. The cerulean sky *aches longingly* under my ballpoint pen. *Amber-colored, deathflies, agate, cataract.*

I'm on my first trip away from home, unless you count a couple of trips to different camps in grade school, which I don't.

There are five travelers, two cars, and a little-used CB channel between us. Though I should, I don't know how to drive yet, so I spend the ride stretched across the backseat of the front car. It's a navy Volvo sedan, and no one but Warren drives it. His roommate John rides shotgun. If I am not working on my terrible poems, I am sketching the hills that lunge past my window.

"Hey." Tony says from the red Corolla bringing up the rear. He and his girlfriend Shelly organized the trip. They work with John and Warren stuffing futon mattresses back in Portland. Tony and Warren and I all went to high school together.

"Hey, man. Hey." Warren says back. They crack one another up like this for hours.

I don't stuff futons. I sleep on a cheap, thin mattress on the floor of a room that the last tenant painted a searing turquoise. I am a twenty-year old art school student and Tony invited me on this trip to act as the photo-journalist.

I have the last line to a poem that I write again and again in the margins of my notebook. *The startling first birds have risen in Utah*; it feels like a last line. I have this sense of myself as a finisher. My third year of college is over, and I've finished it successfully, just like I'll finish college. Like I finished high school. Some days I feel like a dairy cow, waiting for the chute before me to open, so that I know which direction to walk.

But today, I'm riding in the backseat and it feels like floating. I draw a single tire rolling across the stubbled clay I can see beyond the backseat window. The road we're on isn't even on the map bouncing around the backseat with me.

*

The Comb Ridge is loosely west of Bluff, Utah, but it feels like the middle of nowhere. We get there late in the afternoon and set up camp across the highway in the wash, under a hot sun. Tony and Warren refuse to pay for camping, so they drive the cars far enough off the road that they won't be seen.

The rest of the daylight is spent as lizards, draped over rocks, lazily putting tents together, acclimatizing. We have a terrible dinner of undercooked white rice with canned stewed tomatoes ("camping food"), then head to our tents. *I am off the map,* I think. My mother only has a vague notion of where I am. In two days I'll be twenty-one.

At first, it's country-quiet outside. But after only a few moments, intimate murmurs shush from one of the other tents, snoring from another, and the third is silent. Then, the frogs begin to croak and the toads to screech and the sound follows the ribbon of stream off into the canyon. I unzip the side of my sleeping bag, and stretch out like a starfish.

*

The startling first birds have risen in Utah.

The next morning greets us with overcast, low-hanging skies and a steady drizzle. We came from rainy Portland to the parched majestic desert and it looks just like home. At least we aren't afraid of rain.

We pick through prickly pears and soft, gray sagebrush, making our own trail. The sage smells spicy in the wet air and it mixes with the sweet dust of the red clay, which clings to our boots, leaving pink parentheses wherever we climb.

Up one side of a low rock face, there is natural depression, nearly a cave. Inside is a crumbling bricked wall. We scramble up and walk through the rooms, look out someone's thousand-year-old window, stuff our pockets with chips of painted pottery no bigger than pinkie fingernails. Then we slide back down the cliff side squealing through the wetness and starkness of the shrubs and rocks and cacti around us. I take pictures of everyone. I take pictures of the rocks, the bricks, the clouds in the sky. Later, I'll regret the pottery shards, but for today, there is only possibility.

I don't know that in less than three months I will meet the man that, in one more year, I will marry. My life will narrow, the chutes fewer and the walks between them longer. I will get a career, then my marriage will collapse. I will get a house, and then the economy will collapse. Suddenly, with nothing and no one to tether me, it will be just like this again: a wide-open space stretching before me.

*

The startling first birds have risen in Utah.

On the morning of our departure, I wake up early. Rustling comes from the tents, the sounds of spines cracking, stuff sacks being stuffed. Zippers zipping up and down. Lighters flicking against morning cigarettes.

"I'll start the coffee," I hear someone whisper to someone else.

I stand at the edge of our campground in a violet light and inhale the dry perfume of desert air. My eyes trace the routes we have picked through and over the wash, the terrain more familiar now, but still pathless. I make an impossible promise to myself to remember everything.

We are not alone: a tinkling, chicking, and croaking chorus of warblers, wrens, sparrows, and kingbirds bounces wildly around the canyon. It takes a moment, for my ears to adjust to the depth of the sound, like pupils to dim light. From where I stand, it feels like I can hear for miles, the sound progressively more layered and complex. It feels like the entire continent, the whole of the globe, is just this desert, this great expanse. I turn toward camp, I want to explain the birds, the distance, the way that even I feel edgeless, somehow, but everyone is in motion, folding tent poles, fluffing powdered eggs in a skillet, swirling sandy water in yesterday's coffee cups. The moment passes into action and before long, we are packed back into the cars and on the road toward home.

WITH THIS RING

It's on my left ring finger.

It cost a six-pack of Henry Weinhard's beer, one small, potted barrel cactus, and $20. Well, technically, it cost half that because there were two of them. There are still two of them, for all I know.

This kid I knew, Cheyenne, tattooed them for us. He was a couple of years behind me in art school, and was apprenticing with a local tattoo artist, so he'd only asked for twenty bucks. I had to talk my husband into it, but it wasn't a hard sell. The beer was a tip from him and the cactus was a tip from me. I saw online recently that Chey's needle work is in high demand in Portland now.

It's shaped like a simple compass, in black ink. I wanted it to have cardinal points that didn't make it look like a cross. I was very anti-cross back then, though there's no denying the silhouette's resemblance to one. In the center are two semi-circles, crossed arc to arc. Not at all unlike the Chanel logo. But that's a coincidence, too; I've never owned or yearned to own anything Chanel.

Lately, I sometimes see a face in the design. And it's true that the face sometimes looks like the doodle my ex-husband used to draw of himself. But I am ninety-five percent certain that is my mind playing tricks on me, now that I am writing about it and now that the whole question of "removal" has been put on the table.

One man I dated, years after the divorce, said that he could never marry me, since I had "another man's brand" on me. I told him that that said a lot more about him than me, and anyway he needn't worry.

The year I got married, Pamela Anderson and Tommy Lee also got married. Pamela had "Tommy" tattooed on her ring finger, and Tommy got "Pamela" on his. I had not been following Baywatch news at the time, so I had no idea. It's not like we thought we'd made up tattooed wedding rings—but that coincidence was frustrating.

I said, "No, not like them at all," a lot that first year.

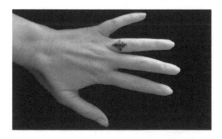

I watched him dance, the night we met. He wasn't any good, but he smiled a lot and I liked that. He had probably looked my way or smiled at me first, for me to be watching him like I was. As each song started to wind down and the pit would begin to wane, I'd make sure I was standing on the edge of the circle right where he'd come out.

It was August 5th, 1994, at Portland's Pine Street Theater, the Cherry Poppin' Daddies were playing an all-ages show. They had a song I liked, that would eventually be a radio hit, called "Shake Your Love Maker." I don't remember anything we said that night. He came home with me, but my little sister was staying over, so we kept our clothes on. That's the big romantic moment we were supposed to relive into our old age.

By the end of that first month, he asked me to marry him, when he thought I was asleep. We did a lot of things like that: on a tightrope between bashful and bold.

The next morning, I said, "Why not?"

Why do I keep it? I've been asked this question a few times over the last fifteen years. It's attached to my body, that's why. Seems a ridiculous question, but I understand that in a world where a C-section can be scheduled for convenience, and a man is planning to have his head transplanted onto a new body, everything seems negotiable. I don't regret that I once felt that way and that when I did, I acted on my feelings. I don't need to see tender pink skin on that finger to know how different I am from the woman who said yes I will yes, once upon a time.

His father was a minister, which for him meant that he had deeply conflicted feelings about church. I didn't go to church. So we agreed, at first, to be very informal about the whole thing. We would travel to Mexico, and when we crossed the border, we'd just be married. We declared it. We'd figure out the details and fill out forms and whatnot later. We did a lot of things like that, too: "later."

There is of course some irony in the fact that a little bit of ink is all that's left of a commitment that was itself supposed to last forever. But even at the time, in some forever-sad part of my heart that learned a broken first language for love a long, long time ago, I knew that even a church wedding doesn't guarantee anything. A piece of paper, a lofty pronouncement, even needling nickel, carbon, and alcohol between layers of skin doesn't obligate anyone to anyone else, not really.

En route to the border, I designed the tattoo, and then, when we walked through the metal gate in San Ysidro, we clenched our hands together and shared a smile and that was it: we were married.

Except of course, we weren't.

I cannot remember whether we got the tattoos before the ceremony, or after.

The ceremony wasn't in my original plan, and we aren't in touch for me to ask him about his, but after two months of telling people, "Well, we are married, just not legally," I agreed to go the whole way. It would just be easier, and it wouldn't change anything between us, I assumed.

Nothing in the known universe lasts forever. It is a childish word. Did I mean for this mark on my finger to signify a great and powerful love for the rest of my life? Of course. Did I mean to keep my promise, made in a ridiculous get-up that included spiral curls, cream-colored lace and hennaed hands, and made as it was before my closest friends and family? Yes. And then I had to break it. If we could predict all the ways in which we might one day fail ourselves and others, I'm not sure how many of us would want to get up the next day.

I made that promise in the best faith I had at the time. I sat still while the needle hummed over my finger and stitched a burning glow under my skin because I believed in my own convictions and I believed that wanting something badly enough would make it manifest.

It was a hot day in August. The fifth, because we thought it was poignant. He was late because he'd left the marriage certificate at home and only remembered halfway there. He was speeding in his borrowed wool tux and our hand-me-down Chrysler LeBaron. We had no "wedding party," just some beloved people hanging out with us and a guy in a black robe in the park. I hadn't known I needed a photographer, so the pictures we collected later were candid and amateurish. One of my uncles, wearing a tie-dyed tank top, took a MiniDV video of the ceremony, but we had no way to watch it, and it's since been lost.

When the groom is late to the wedding, people cannot help but make nervous jokes about it. But I was never in any doubt. He dropped a lot of balls, but back then—and this is the entire reason (I believe now) that I went through with it at all—I knew I wouldn't be one of them.

As far as the tattoos, I went first, to show him how quick and relatively painless it would be. I already had four, on my ankle and shoulders, and he had none. The tattoo has always seemed to me to be a symbol for the things I liked to do at the time. I know this is callous, and that's my burden to carry, too, but he was one of the things I liked to do at the time. So was getting tattooed.

It had been so long since I'd had regular contact with my father that I didn't even realize we'd chosen his birthday for our wedding date. That fact plays no material role in our short marriage, but I wonder now if a part of me knew we were doomed from the beginning. Did I try, then, to etch a permanence that I suspected would elude us both?

I spent a lot of time looking at my finger in the weeks of healing that followed and then, too, in the years that followed. On the surface, a healing tattoo looks like any other superficial wound: there is some blood, then a scab, which in the case of black ink tattoos takes on the black, and when the dark scab falls off on its own, instead of pink skin beneath, as you might expect given the shade of the scab, there are smooth black lines below. This is because the ink is both above and below the surface. During the act of tattooing, one or several mechanized needles are used to push the pigments under the first layer of the skin to the second. There, the body recognizes the ink as an invasive substance, but the particles of ink are not carried away like a speck of bacteria would be or wood fiber from a papercut. Instead, the ink stays more or less in place, underneath the dermis (the layer of skin that is constantly turning over). For a long time, it was assumed that the pigment stayed put because of the size of the ink particles.

It was quick and relatively painless, like I'd said it would be, just like crossing the border had been, just like getting married had been—one year exactly from the date of that 'Daddies show—just like how, eventually, leaving him would be.

Another man's brand. As though this thing: my idea, my drawing, my friend the tattoo artist, my—there's no denying—insistence, belongs to anyone other than me. As though the guy asking me about it didn't keep his own old wedding band in a box by his bed. This ring is my own signature. It says that I was there.

I was there when it was good and I was there when it was bad. For the long hikes into the Olympics, the Tetons, the Sandias, and for the long weeks between paydays, all the grocery money drunk away.

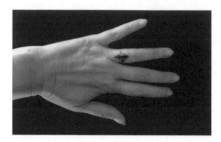

I was there when he drove home so wasted he let the car run out of gas in the middle of the road, two blocks from our house and needed my help, in the middle of the night, to push it home. When I had to leave work early, bus across town, and argue with a bartender about closing his tab—because he'd left his own wallet at home. I told work it was a family emergency, not that my husband was calling from a bar. My manager had already had to give me rides home after midnight on the nights he drank too much to remember to pick me up.

And I was there when we danced through the streets at Mardi Gras, giving away pot cookies and laughing so hard my sides hurt for days. I was there when he taught me to dice an onion, pack peanut butter and jelly tortillas for hiking. I was there for all the live music in all the towns we saw together. That time the mushrooms came on just as the Beastie Boys took the stage. That terrible Melvins show, that was still good, somehow. I was there on the other side of the performance line at the jazz club where he worked, ordering appetizers and beers, stretching out my stay, watching him do the one thing he was great at doing: tossing a sauté pan effortlessly, charring filet mignons and perfectly searing tuna steaks.

What I had wanted, so badly, was a light and fun love. I wanted laughter and adventure and none of the screaming and yelling that I'd known so much of, first between my parents and later, between my stepfather and me. I wanted to be healed, though I didn't know of what at the time. And what he wanted, I can speculate from the clues we left behind in our dueling escapes, was to lead an adventure without having any responsibility for its success.

After a while, my own depression and anxiety, like his addiction, began to fill the spaces between escapades. My circular frantic thoughts told me that I would never get anywhere if I had to spend my days bailing him out of his mishaps. Apologizing for bounced checks. Making excuses for missed appointments. Paying impound fees. While unhelpful, those thoughts weren't wrong.

The truth of the end is as unromantic as the truth of the beginning. Nothing ever did change—not his drinking, not my sadness—and that became the standard I carried into every battle we had, large and small. Until one day, after practicing how I'd say it, I said I was done. I had to talk him into it, but it wasn't a hard sell, either.

For a moment, one recent spring, I seriously considered having it removed. I told myself that it would make things easier. And by things I meant the new relationship I was in and possibly the next new relationship, and checking out at the grocery store and depositing money at the bank and standing in line for a movie.

These are all places where people can see my hand, and many of them ask me questions about it. For years, I've felt compelled to answer, every time, out of politeness.

I never ask anyone about their tattoos unless they bring them up first.

I made an appointment at an office, or perhaps it was technically a "spa," equipped with a variety of lasers. You could laser away wrinkles or inches off your waist or acne scars or bad tattoos there. They had a Groupon.

The way the laser is supposed to work on tattoos is that the pinpoint of light goes through the dermis to the pigment particles and one by one zaps each particle into smaller pieces that the body's immune system can more effectively process. Like a game of Asteroids at the cellular level. But results vary greatly.

The whole visit lasted about 4 minutes. I spoke with a woman in a long white jacket who was wearing way too much makeup to work in any environment that required a lab coat. She said it might cost as much as $300 beyond what I'd already paid—perhaps even a bit more— to have the black ink substantially dimmed, possibly to the point of imperceptibility. She noted that black ink was the hardest to remove.

There could be some mild scarring, but everyone's skin responded to the laser differently, she'd said.

I wondered, but did not ask, if I could get a second Groupon to have any tattoo-removal scars removed by the scar-erasing laser.

It was too much. I left. Not just the money, but the whole thing. The cheesy office, the imperfect promise, the mood of the conversation called to mind words like blemish and mistake. Neither of those felt accurate. But then what was I hoping to accomplish by zapping the nickeled ink out from under my dermis?

What gets erased if the laser does its job? I know, not the memories. But something is lost, and I am not sure it would be the right thing.

This is not a scientific study, but I'd hazard that nine out of ten cashiers really like my ring finger tattoo. So many of them are young, and so sometimes I say, "Don't ever do it" with a smile I hope is wry. I can't even say, "Think of Tommy and Pamela," anymore because they don't know who they are.

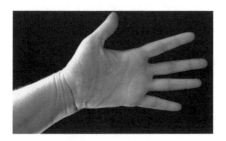

A brand. Who thinks like that? Someone with a red-hot iron in his hands, I'd guess.

I don't think I keep it as a cautionary tale. But I do think that's what worries some of these men I've loved in the many years since: the idea that I might not fall for their nonsense, having proof of the trouble it can lead to. My own fickle nature makes it hard for me to not consider, at least, that it's a valid worry.

And yet, even if I am too cynical in addition to callous now, maybe I like to recollect a time when I wasn't. Because it's true: there are days when I am tired of what the ring represents to everyone else. That it can't ever be anything new, that it will always be "my wedding ring." And on those days, too, I am tired of what the ring reminds me of.

There's a lot I've forgotten, like how we got to Mexico when our car was broke down, like what song we danced to at the reception, like what his last words were to me, barely 5 years later, in his crummy new apartment in Santa Fe, two months after we split up. I thought he would be an anchor for me. That was my mistake. He was still sinking when I found him and my heart was too heavy.

There's a lot I remember, too: I crossed that border twenty years ago, and I jumped with open arms into a terrible idea. There were many good days. I don't want to be left with a scar instead of my own scrawl. I don't want my desire for absolution to be the thing I see in some smudged shadow of charcoal from the carbon left behind, or a bubbling keloid—everyone's skin responds differently after all.

There is, of course, a third option between the ring going or staying—that of covering it up, transforming the points into something else, a star or the stamens of a flower, perhaps. Setting the swirl of carrier and heavy metals upon itself to alchemize a new meaning for me. Pamela had her tattoo artist turn the cursive "Tommy" on her finger into "Mommy." Tommy said in an interview he had his removed.

But even twenty years later, I don't quite know what meaning I want or need or deserve, perched there, just above the edge of the palm of my hand. I used to be so sure, and that surety allowed me a blithe recklessness whose loss I mourn now more than any love.

"How long were you married?" As though the answer says anything about being married. When I had a house, everyone wanted to know what I paid for it. There's something about numbers that tell us what we want to know about a thing, more than anything intrinsic to the thing itself. Like this tattoo. It's not the marriage. It's proof that a marriage happened. It's proof that once I had a great deal of hope in forever. There are days when that is a balloon that can carry me away and days when the weight of it threatens to pin me to the ground.

The black lines are blurred, now. The negative spaces between them are shrinking, and my finger skin (my finger skin!) is creped and wrinkled in a way I never imagined at 22. I can only clearly see the design I drew when I curl my fingers all the way under my palm and stretch my skin like a canvas. The longest edges still point forward and back.

Science has recently discovered that tattoos last as long as they do because a particular type of cell in the immune system, called a macrophage, stores and then bequeaths the ink. The first macrophage gobbles the ink as it would any invader but then when the cell dies, instead of the ink being released to the blood stream or carried away to the lymph nodes the way a sliver or bacteria would be, the ink is taken up by another macrophage and carried until cell death.

A tattoo isn't a stain or blemish, then, so much as a process. It doesn't pin your skin down in time, but is a thing that changes, cell by cell the way everything else in the world does. In the end (which the structure of an essay requires, even as the living of life resists), it doesn't matter if I laser away the darkest ink or leave it or cloak it in a floral swirl—I will always know the mark that's there just under the surface, moving in and out of my cells and my memory.

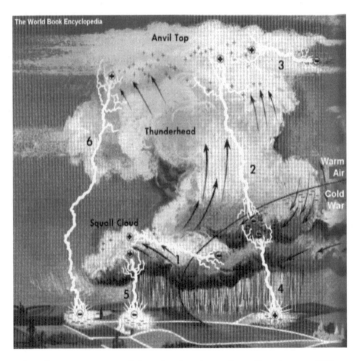

Lightning is a monsoon visitor in the American Southwest. When the sun becomes a weight upon our backs, when our tongues swell and throats crack, when the summer must break, then the storm clouds come, like Spanish galleons sailing across the landscape. All in one motion, our hands shield our eyes and we glare past the heat ripples at the horizon. We try to calculate the storm's arrival: ground temperature times wind speed divided by our combined thirst.

Shelter is easily won in the city. But on the town's perimeter, where nothing's taller than a cactus, lightning will come in blinding, terrifying bursts. Everywhere ungrounded ground unfurls. In the desert, jackrabbits, geckos, wrens and mockingbirds flee the storm cloud in panicked flurries. But their paths are wayward—they run in zigzags, like the lightning itself—because there is no easy prediction for away, where lightning is concerned, only the surety of the fluttering animal heart that here is no longer safe.

Before it arrives, a hot wind blows, strong enough to topple yard chairs and spin roof chickens dizzy. Mothers call through the park, beckoning their children home. We turn our backs to the storm, to the grit, as neighborhood cats twist under spiked and tangled mesquite limbs; under porch awnings, dogs lower their bellies to the Saltillo tile. Sparrows spiral out of cottonwood trees and loop down to hide in the bright bougainvillea vines near the foundations of homes.

We turn to watch the white legs of the cumulonimbus blasting from the sky as boned roots, burning black tracks in the sand. In the distance, the ships rumble closer.

The cloud seems like such a solid, finite shape, but always, we miss its edge. The daylight empurples as the wind swirls wet, warm and directionless. And then it's upon us—we're under the sweating belly, the dancing feet kniving between the houses. Our hairs lift just before the breathtaking roar, as though they would meet the bolt halfway if they could. As though we could climb this ghost bone to heaven.

Each flash illuminates the storm-marauded streets and yards. The light, so bright and fast, throws everything into afterimage: along the stone fence, pale silhouettes of saguaro, and black water rocking the kidney-shaped pool. Somewhere down the block, the shockwave sets off a car alarm. The only other sound we hear is the storm sound: rain crashing and the wind's force.

The air stays charged after a strike. The electricity ripples through fat raindrops, across the now leaf-strewn pool, among the leathery palm leaves, along power lines, over houses. We are in the middle of it. And then a bolt hits closer. The neighbor's shed is split open: the walls become aluminum petals, the yard tools, pistils and stamens, all scattered in submission. It is near enough that the sound of the thunder and the force of the electrical charge boom in unison. We feel it between our heart and ribs. In this space we are animals—we have the urge to flight: *RUN RUN RUN*, which fights every line of logic we learned as children. *Are we grounded? Are we conductive?*

Lightning splits the moment into before and after. Before is taut, possible. After, you realize that, at some moment, your breath stopped in your throat, waiting. We watch, our eyebrows pinched up, along with the cats, and geckos, and dogs and sparrows. We lose count of the blue-white strikes. We whisper one-one-thousand, two-one-thousand, three-one-thousand as the space between light and sound lengthens, until the clouds are again in the distance, only now, moving away.

And then we let out a long-held breath.

PART VI:: SONG CRYSTALLIZATION

BONE

Great flocks of late summer vultures circle campus, worrying the incoming freshmen.

The birds coast on thermal air currents, spiraling first up, and then, in wider and wider circles, back down. Adults teach the fledglings by example to conserve energy, to stretch their wings wide and rock along the rising bubbles of warm air, rather than flap. The lessons are quiet, graceful. As autumn takes over Laramie, the shorter days will mean less sun to heat the ground; the thermal columns will be fewer, and the birds will move south. And who among us hasn't longed to escape one winter or another?

When the vultures leave, the job of clean-up will be handed back to the resident crows and ravens, who noisily announce even the smallest fortune. New World vultures have no syrinx, or vocal chords. They hiss in alarm and grunt or whine for any other need. And while

I can see over a dozen from my office right now, I've yet to see them hunched and flocked around any of the local roadkill: rabbits and squirrels who, in a moment of bravery, sought the other side of the street and failed. But neither have I ever seen a two-day old carcass. The birds are modest in their efficiency.

And their efficiency is admirable. It takes only five hours for a flock of Turkey vultures to dispatch the soft tissue on an adult human corpse. We have forensic science to thank for that bit of trivia, useful for interrogating what remains of us, in certain desert landscapes, for the missing time between lost and found.

The term vulture comes from the Greek word, vulturus, or "tearer." Turkey vultures have a weak grip: they use their talons, not to tear, but to hold bones down in the dust so the real work can be done with their sharp, curved beaks. We call them scavenger, but this is too unsympathetic a word for the service they provide. They dispatch that which horrifies us so that we might imagine, for a moment, a world where all rabbits are safe, where all roads are crossable. With their heads jammed down in the literal heart of the matter, they tear and rip and shred until every pliable, awful scrap is gone, and only hard whiteness remains—here a thigh bone no longer connected to a hip bone, there a mouth still full of teeth, the tongue long gone. Without vultures, "'Close to the bone' would fall out of use as a measure of sharply felt truth" says Lia Purpura, in her essay "On Coming Back as a Buzzard." Close to the bone is not a comfortable place to be. Close to the bone is where the hardest truths lie.

In my grandmother's *National Geographic Field Guide to the Birds of North America*, 1983 edition, she's made four marks next to the Turkey vulture entry. A check mark next to the bird's name means that at some point in the twenty-odd years that she kept track, she saw one. A small star under the check means that she saw one on her property in Estacada, Oregon. The property that is now, years later, mine. Based on the map next to the description, the bird she saw was probably there enjoying the temperate summer like Laramie's vultures. It would disappear south before the first hard frost.

Just underneath the map she's written what might be a letter V and an M. I think the M stands for *many* or *multiple*, but I don't know for sure. Perhaps the V means "various sites." Every page in the guide looks like this: painted plates of birds on each right-facing page, and maps, text, and her notes on the left.

The last time I saw her alive, I asked my grandmother about these marks. Other birds in the book have the same VM (which might be a "check-M") and some, just an M. Some have circled capital A's nearby. Sometimes the penciled mark was inked over in blue or black pen. There are also occasional dates and place names noted in the margins or along the top of the page. She saw her first Green jay in Texas, in February of 1988, her hasty scrawl informs me. She used to write down every bird she saw every day—but she can't remember where in her towers of papers and books those journals are hidden. They're somewhere; she won't throw a single thing away. I was welcome to look for them, she said. But the task of searching felt Herculean. I regretted the brevity of my visit, my fear of the large country spiders that guard her things now, her drifting attention. She couldn't remember what the M stands for, or the possible V.

*

I saw my grandmother for the first time in years because my mother said it might be the last chance I'd get. The women in my family tend to live longer than expected, despite a proclivity to histrionics, so I thought she was exaggerating. But I'd been away for years, and this seemed as good a reason to visit as any, so I got in the car and drove twenty hours for a picnic.

It was like this. My parents, my mother's oldest brother, his wife, and I have come to visit, this improbable August, because of word from my youngest uncle that my grandmother's health is failing fast. If she were more alert, she might ask why we are all here, with no holiday and no birthday to celebrate. It is a somber party, to be sure, whose dissembled meaning is not lost on my grandfather. Though his legs shake violently if he stands too long, he gets up to greet each guest at the door as they arrive: his sister, my soldier cousin, his wife, their son, family friends, and still more tenuous relations, until the house is full.

In her backyard, we have a picnic, which, for the first time in my life, my grandmother does not prepare. Everyone chips in, recreating her dishes. My mother makes the deviled eggs while my aunt worries aloud about the lack of MSG for the potato salad. Grandma used it as her secret ingredient in just about everything and the food won't taste right without it. It has been a long time since my last trip home.

At one point, from her wheelchair in the grass, she says my name and my sister's name to my mother.

Yes, my mother says loudly, then she repeats our names back to my grandmother.

I can remember them just fine when they're together, my grandmother says. But I've been having a lot of trouble with names lately. The names of everything.

My sister isn't here, but at her home in Arizona. My mother just nods. It doesn't feel like Alzheimer's, my grandmother says, later in the afternoon. She hasn't forgotten how to act or who she is (like her father did, at the end), just words, names. Her bluntness is meant to inform, not comfort.

Throughout the afternoon a mood of assessment runs through her children's behavior. They will discuss in hushed tones, later, that it's hard not to think about logistics. The stacks of things that need to be parsed. The garage, oh god, the garage! Who is willing to tear through the spiders, to find that which was promised to whomever, however long ago? Who among them can bear to separate the skin of a life from the bones of its house? There is no financial urgency—my grandmother's things are worth little—but one of longing: growing up under this roof was not easy, and a few good memories are frozen in picture frames, puppy figurines, and chipped china.

I don't remember her as a still person, or a static one, as she is today, stuck in her chair. She dyed her hair chestnut until I was in college and had a once-impressive collection of matching pantsuits—all the better for clambering over fences for the perfect shot of an old barn, or tromping through the brush collecting dried seed pods. After retiring from a short career as a receptionist at her small town's only doctor's office, she traveled the world with my grandfather to look for birds, among other things. She brought back photos of kookaburras, toucans, and white cranes. Today, my grandfather tells us, is the first time she's been outside in weeks. Her white hair sticks out from her head at odd angles, as her matchstick legs do from a limp house-dress draped and fluttering around her. She used to criticize my weight, my clothes, my smile. Now, I feel only a perplexing pain and ferocity both—and a deep sadness over this preoccupation with appearances that has her, even now, patting down her own rogue hairs and tugging at her hem.

Once she's settled back in the living room, a process that takes several minutes as well as the help of my uncle and a wheeled-walker, I ask her what her favorite bird is. She grasps at the air with her hands, small and bird-like themselves now. I can't tell whether she has a favorite and can't recall its name or if she can't pick from the thousands she's seen and longed to see. I open one of her old field guides and turn to the Evening grosbeak. I remember her trying to lure them to her feeder when I was younger. It's on the last plate, and its name has both a check and a star on the opposite page. She slides her glasses up and down the tip of her nose until she can focus on the images.

Oh, those are everywhere now, she says, dismissing them. She stares at the other birds, one by one. Her whole head moves to center each painting within the range of her telescoped vision. Below the grosbeak are a male and female bullfinch. She lets go of the book with her right hand and it sags. I grab it, take the weight of it for her, and she shakily points to a bullfinch.

I saw that one in Germany, she states, and moves her glasses back up. She looks toward the picture window and the bird feeders out in her yard for a moment, then shakes her head a little. The book forgotten, she turns to the television, her face blank. In the left page margin, under Eurasian bullfinch (listed as a rare migrant) is a check mark, and in black pen it says, "84 GER."

*

Back at my desk in Laramie, I watch the dark shapes circle up, then down. They epitomize patience as they wait for air currents, the slowest rabbit, the reckless squirrel.

I'm supposed to be writing up my summer research on beetles and oysters, but the vultures can't wait their turn. In an ironic twist, I devour all I can about them—information and photographs of vultures all over the world. I tell myself that it is an ornithological, an ecological, a scientific fascination. But I stack these facts up to hide behind while a wave of loss threatens. The women in my family all live such long lives, after all, and I want the chance to talk again to my grandmother about birds. An impossible hope, I know, as her mind is sliding in only one direction, now.

Their defense against predators is to vomit rotten meat. Their gastric juices can destroy anthrax. With a wingspan of over 10 feet, the Eurasian black vulture is the world's largest raptor and is most at home in the Chinese and Mongolian steppes. A livestock drug that has killed nearly all of India's vultures is now being marketed in Africa.

I learn from a couple of European papers that governmental concern over Mad Cow Disease has led to laws requiring that farmers incinerate their dead livestock. With less carrion available to them, they say, the Spanish vultures have turned predatory. No longer content to wait for the final scene, the birds are forcing the denouement. They are, hysterical farmers and the hungry journalists covering them report, especially fond of newborn calves.

A vulture's got to eat, too, I think. If our own brave, street-crossing prey were to vanish, exterminated under a new urban management plan, or by a sudden influx of owls, who here would take their place? If it meant one had to lie down upon the yellow line and wait?

I read an essay long ago on rescuing vultures, and the writer said that she would welcome "burial" by vulture because it would mean becoming a part of its flight. A lovely, if ridiculous sentiment. I doubt she would volunteer in an imperiled calves' place, since dying, to be sure, is nothing like already dead.

As I write this, later still, my grandmother is already dead.

I flip through the field guide, force myself to remember each of those years, what she looked like then, where I was—as though re-telling myself were an antidote to the slow dive down into confusion that is my likely inheritance. There are notes from beaches she took me to, towns we drove past in summers when I was a child.

I consider adding my own message next to the Turkey vulture, maybe "UWyo 12." But I can't quite bring the pen down to the page. I have my own birding guide, a new copy of Sibley's, which has remained notation-free so far. Would my experience, today's view of vultures, be less of an intrusion between its crisp pages?

In the end, indecision rather than any kind of reverence stays my hand. I don't know what mark would bring this day back forty years from now, which careful combination of letters and numbers could get my mind across those years in one piece. Or, if by then, that's even what I'd want. To remember everything—by which I mean all the slights, embarrassments, rules, and losses that edge darkly any life along with the good—might be worse. When my own neural networks begin to tangle and the connections break, I will not get to choose what will stay and what will vanish. And picking at that fear like a loose thread is folly. Instead, I'd rather stare down any eye that would keep me from leaping bravely into the road. Even that dark red-ringed eye which will one day see my bones in the dust and think, Now, it is over. Because at least for today, for this hour, for this breath, it is not.

PYROLOGY // an account(ing)*

On the sidewalk, at dusk: the head of a razor, a plastic filter from a cigarillo, and other unconnected, broken pieces of lives.[1]

122°F on June 26, 1990;

121°F on July 28, 1995;

120°F on June 25, 1990;

119°F on June 29, 2013;

118°F on July 16, 1925;

118°F June 24, 1929;

118°F July 11, 1958;

118°F July 4, 1989;

118°F June 27, 1990;

118°F June 28, 1990;

118°F July 27, 1995;

118°F July 21, 2006;

118°F July 2, 2011;

I SUPPOSE NO MAN EVER SAW NIAGARA FOR THE FIRST TIME WITHOUT FEELING DISAPPOINTED. I SUPPOSE NO MAN EVER SAW IT THE FIFTH TIME WITHOUT WONDERING HOW HE COULD EVER HAVE BEEN SO BLIND AND STUPID AS TO FIND ANY EXCUSE FOR DISAPPOINTMENT IN THE FIRST PLACE. I SUPPOSE THAT ANY ONE OF NATURE'S MOST CELEBRATED WONDERS WILL ALWAYS LOOK RATHER INSIGNIFICANT TO A VISITOR AT FIRST, BUT ON A BETTER ACQUAINTANCE WILL SWELL AND STRETCH OUT AND SPREAD ABROAD, UNTIL IT FINALLY GROWS CLEAR BEYOND HIS GRASP - BECOMES TOO STUPENDOUS FOR HIS COMPREHENSION.

---

*   Includes text from Mark Twain published in the Sacramento *Daily Union*, November 16, 1866.

1   I sat outside in the steam, through monsoon rains, counting thunder and lightning, back when I was a smoker, back when I was a wife.

Ticking, like the stone clocks under every mountain. Breaking, like moonlight through someone else's beige blinds. A hum, hard to place[2]

1991 – Mount Pinatubo;

1980 – Mount St. Helens;

1912 – Novarupta;

1902 – Santa María;

1886 – Mount Tarawera;

1883 – Krakatoa;

1835 – Cosigüina;

1815 – Mount Tambora;

1783 – Grímsvötn;

1650 – Kolumbo, Santorini;

1600 – Kuaynaputina;

1580 – Billy Mitchell;

1477 – Bárðarbunga;

1452 – Kuwae;

1280 – Quilotoa.

THE GREATER PART OF THE VAST FLOOR OF THE DESERT UNDER US WAS AS BLACK AS INK, AND APPARENTLY SMOOTH AND LEVEL; BUT OVER A MILE SQUARE OF IT WAS RINGED AND STREAKED AND STRIPED WITH A THOUSAND BRANCHING STREAMS OF LIQUID AND GORGEOUSLY BRILLIANT FIRE! IT LOOKED LIKE A COLOSSAL RAILROAD MAP OF THE STATE OF MASSACHUSETTS DONE IN CHAIN LIGHTNING ON THE MIDNIGHT SKY. IMAGINE IT - IMAGINE A COAL-BLACK SKY SHIVERED INTO A TANGLED NETWORK OF ANGRY FIRE!

---

2   It doesn't do any good to remember the exact smoothness of your shoulder; but it snowed last night and my room is cold.

Every spring fails by autumn. What I'm saying is that maybe the problem is with the word itself.[3]

2005 – M—;

2012 – T—;

2008 – Y—;

2000 – A—;

1990 – S—;

1992 – A—;

1994 – D—;

1993 – A—;

1991 – B—;

1992 – M—;

2011 – J—;

2010 – J—;

2009 – R—;

1989 – J—;

1987 – P—.

I FORGOT TO SAY THAT THE NOISE MADE BY THE BUBBLING LAVA IS NOT GREAT, HEARD AS WE HEARD IT FROM OUR LOFTY PERCH. IT MAKES THREE DISTINCT SOUNDS - A RUSHING, A HISSING, AND A COUGHING OR PUFFING SOUND; AND IF YOU STAND ON THE BRINK AND CLOSE YOUR EYES IT IS NO TRICK AT ALL TO IMAGINE THAT YOU ARE SWEEPING DOWN A RIVER ON A LARGE LOW PRESSURE STEAMER, AND THAT YOU HEAR THE HISSING OF THE STEAM ABOUT HER BOILERS, THE PUFFING FROM HER ESCAPE PIPES AND THE CHURNING RUSH OF THE WATER ABAFT HER WHEEL. THE SMELL OF SULFUR IS STRONG, BUT NOT UNPLEASANT TO A SINNER.

---

3   It is easy to box your things: letters, photos, mix tapes. But now I see you in the lines around my eyes—where can I put those?

NOTES TOWARD
A PARTIAL DEFINITION OF HOME

I almost always arrive a stranger. I drive up with what I can carry and carve out a space for myself. Austin. Rockville. Phoenix. Laramie. Sheridan. Hamilton.

There is an attempt to establish ties. Then, there is somewhere else. I say that it's my work, my calling, my spirit. But really, no place has held me so close that I couldn't walk away. No place has come for me after I decided to go. It is, perhaps, too much to ask of a place.

*

Most towns are designed with liminal spaces, and those that aren't acquire them over time. These spaces are the looser boundaries that edge the more civilized centers of neighborhoods and cities. The shaded path around the golf course, the "greenbelt," the farthest rows of the rose garden, the copse by the buggy lake, the reclaimed river walk. Streets and shops and intersections are too loud, busy, and fast for any initial insights, so the borderlands can afford a slower entry. One learns little in the middle of the action, except how to dodge and deflect, because in their bustling hearts, towns most resemble one another.

Nature is obdurate in these half-wild places. Much can be learned of the blind desire to thrive despite less than ideal conditions that can be seen where what has been made or built begins to unravel. Weeds exploit cracks, vines climb any post driven. Wildflowers curl from under the edges of boards. Beetles, bees, snakes, spiders, seek out whatever we've left behind and make their homes there. This growing-despite can look like freedom.

*

When I told my husband that we were done, I remember saying, "This isn't working. We aren't, I mean, and I'm tired of trying." It came out faster than I'd meant for it to and he didn't believe me. Not at first. He asked, "What now?" and also, "Can't we just buy something to make this better?" (We had a lot of debt.) He said, "We could plan some trip somewhere." (We had tried that, too.) And he said, "Is this about," but he didn't finish, because he didn't know what it could be about. (There was a woman once, and I'd always wondered, but it wasn't about her, or his drinking, exactly.)

In my mind's eye, I can see us moving from the bedroom through the living room and into the kitchen, the full length of our small space, but I don't remember what I said, how he responded. I know I'd been practicing the moment for weeks.

*

These in-betweens, these micro-geographies can be a welcomed respite from the hassles and small sorrows that accompany frequent moves: connecting the utilities; registering your body, your car, your rights; the favorite cup, now broken; the lost box of ornaments. Though the terrain might be steep and basaltic, or red-clayed and rolling like the waves that once overlaid it, and the landscape may sprout ferns as big as a VW bug or sticky cholla or fluted and waxy canna blooms, there is always something reliable, something gentle and untended about the curve of the walkways. You can walk at a pace of your choosing, and it is difficult to get lost or stray too far from landmarks you might recently have learned.

*

We'd only been in Santa Fe a year. I'd hoped the desert air might dry out something that had grown damp in us, but like a water stain, the mark of dissatisfaction remained. I walked out of the house after I told him.

I'd only ever left the house like that once before, back in Portland, when I thought for a moment that I wouldn't marry him at all. That night, I waited at a park nearby for an hour, in the dark and the rain, sobbing dramatically on the rubber seat of a playground swing set. I dug two deep ruts with my heels in the sodden chipped wood. I was waiting for him to come find me. He never did. It was a childish game, but the only one I knew at the time.

So now walking down the hill away from our half of the 150-year old adobe we rented, I knew I could walk in peace; I knew he would not come for me. I felt something give in my hips, a shift with each step. I felt the precise way my feet planted themselves on the uneven stone sidewalk, then peeled up and away from it. I felt how the steps made my spine twist back and forth like a chain might, in a light wind. My arms swept heavy from my shoulders, propelling me forward. By concentrating on just that act of walking, I kept something else from happening. I walked past xeriscaped gardens and villas behind stucco walls, past spent agaves. Past clumps of prickly pear. I was not crying, but gulping at the air, like a fish. I remember the way the dust motes held still in the air while I tried

[I did try.]

while I tried to be sure. At the bottom of the hill, I called a friend, who met me at the only bar in town worth anything. She and I often played pool there, and it felt like a safe place to be torn in half. So then I was: I wept on the couch for hours and the bartenders bought my beers. It felt very grown up, very battered-by-life, at the time.

∗

As I walk the edges of a new place, I try to learn the names of its trees, but I often fail after one or two. It's easier for me to learn the habits of its birds.

- In Phoenix, the mockingbirds would direct traffic, sparrows would shyly follow me down the block, in case I was in a generous mood.

- In New Orleans, all I remember hearing were starlings, screaming like car alarms in the middle of the night, and the one morning when the first cardinal I'd ever seen surprised me with his unmistakable red hood in the small tree in front of my house.

- In Portland, there were robins and house sparrows everywhere in the city, in the marshy spaces on the edge of town, red-winged black birds, herons, ducks, while deep in the woods, there were owls, woodpeckers.

Only certain birds can be at home in our landscape of cement, iron, and fiberglass. Pigeons are especially resilient, bedding down in the S-curves of neon signs, or the joints of tin-shingled overhangs. Some swallows, long drawn by the gnats and midges our trash breeds, make mud nests under freeway overpasses or high arching entranceways, where once they favored tall river banks and barns. These birds can teach a person how to make the best of things.

Other birds give a different lesson entirely: to follow the pull of migration, to move or perish.

*

And then, when he thought he understood, there in the kitchen, his shoulders bowed but his face hidden, my husband agreed to go. Many days later, when he thought he understood better, he refused.

He insisted then, angry and full of his own practiced speech, that if I wanted to be alone so badly, I should go somewhere and be alone, then. I don't know if that was his way of asking me to stay, but maybe it was. He knew I hated to be alone. For once, I did not hold his anger against him. For once, I felt a small tenderness toward his weaknesses.

*

Walking around the overgrown hedgerows of a new town, you can get a picture of the people who live nearby, your new, as-yet unmet neighbors, through their trash or their fastidiousness, through the well-worn or neglected nature of their paths. It's not a fair judgment, but it is nonetheless an easy first one to make. It's a side-long glance you can take without being caught.

*

He will always look the same in my memory: he's dancing terribly at an all-ages show in jeans cut off and cuffed at the knee, black boots, and a flannel shirt, and for this (and maybe also his ridiculous wide-toothed grin), I pick him out from the other thrashing bodies in the pit.

When each song ends, I make sure I am nearby, even though his long hair is on the way out of style. Even though he is too tall and too skinny. Over and over again, I pick him out.

*

New Orleans is slowly being overtaken by kudzu, one fence and one doorway at a time. The flowers there are decadent and wanton, overflowing their hanging baskets and window boxes like the Quarter itself.

Oak trees tower over Mid-City, gnarled and indefatigable, like the great old barons and baronesses of yore. But the joke's on history, because the barons are dead, their power, finally being eroded like the delta they tried to master, while the trees abide.

The great Mississippi flows stinking rot and massive steel hulls past the city's reinforced flanks. Sometimes, the river climbs the banks, wild and unimpressed with our constructs, reminding everyone whose land they live upon.

At night, the smells of cayenne, cheap beer, and vomit on Decatur Street mingle in the humid air, while cicadas and brass bands keep time.

Who, who wasn't born up out of the damp loam here, like a cypress or morning glory, could imagine building a home on its uneven, sinking surfaces?

Or, what was I ever thinking? My shoes grew mold. My drawings rotted in my portfolio case. There were fleas and mosquitoes everywhere. I was cruel and petty in response to cruelty and pettiness.

I did not know what I was doing.

*

The more a person moves, the easier moving becomes. Leaving, however, is not the same as moving.

*

It was never perfect, not even at first. I hold no illusions. We fought badly and never apologized. We took everything that we built or drew toward us for granted. For my part, I lost respect for his ability to lead us. He lost faith in my ability to make a home for us.

So to be clear, it was not the loss of perfection that I mourned as I walked down the hill, gasping last or first breaths. It was something else, something that I haven't quite reached yet. It feels like a thing waiting around the next bend, a kind of understanding that might bring me some peace.

*

There is a release in the air on paths that mark the space between homes and not-homes, a kind of collective human exhale. These spaces are not exactly our spaces, and any people walking these paths are visitors, even if they come every day. The trees, the moving water and the still, the hidden, calling birds—have little need of us. I can be released here of the burden of my intractable nature.

*

In Portland, in 1995, the waitlist for a summer wedding in Shakespeare's rose garden was nearly two years long. If we'd waited that long, what might have happened? We picked the rhododendron garden instead, because there was no wait. The flowers weren't even in bloom. I walked across a short lawn to meet him and a Justice of the Peace by a park bench. A few of our friends and family stood around squinting in the late summer light, their cheeks sun-reddened and balled up with smiles.

Not too many months later, we packed our shared belongings

and moved to New Orleans. It took us over a year to get there, but that's a story about the middle of a thing. I'm talking here about its outer edges.

*

The American Rhododendron Society describes rhododendrons as shallow-rooted. They do not tolerate soils that are allowed to grow stagnant with moisture.

*

Maybe what I've lost isn't a place or time at all, but a belief in the integrity of the moment before any real loss was imaginable (of respect, of faith), that moment when a long, imperfect history lay before us because we'd sworn it would be so.

*

I said we were done in June, two months before our 5-year anniversary. He stood at the sink with his back to me and washed his cooks' knives. It was not an intimidating act on his part, but a defensive one: washing knives was a thing he knew how to do well, arguing with me was not. He was so tall, that he had to lean over to reach the water. I don't know if his shoulders were curved down in defeat or in diligence.

I remember nothing else of the month that followed, except walking down the hill with its paused motes, and an old friend coming to town from far away, to spend the last few nights with me in the house my husband and I had shared.

Was I cruel? If I was, it was unintentional. I got drunk at the bar over a game of pool with my local friend and my out of town friend and I cried great choking sobs that turned into laughter. I shouted drunkenly about the irony of my hating my husband's drinking. I put my head on the green felt and thought I might die. It was my way of asking them not to go. I didn't want anyone to go, ever again. I remind myself, now, that I was still very young then. I remind myself that I was the one leaving. Who leaves.

*

Birds have their own ideas about what makes a marriage successful or useful. Song birds, for example, are rarely monogamous for more than a single season.

*

I'm not trying to say I'm anything like a song bird. I'm not trying to say anything about the institution of marriage, or my disposition for it. I'm trying to say that sometimes it's easier to describe one's arc far from the heart of things.

*

New Mexico is rich with yellow and red sandstones, sage, and twisted, spiked mesquite. The cactus there blooms after rain. The desert scrub is full of thrashers and quail and roadrunners. Rotten wood and quartz-streaked stones hide a menagerie of venomous creatures. As you climb the great highway from Albuquerque to Santa Fe, the hills darken with puffed and pointed foliage, until the tree-line demarcates the start of ski slopes. Hawks circle overhead. There are small pines and lavish pink bougainvillea climbing pueblo walls.

*

It would be disingenuous to be even a little vague about the burden my unhappiness was to us both. Though he might have stayed from habit or duty, there was not much worth staying for by the time we'd reached Santa Fe.

*

Some cities hold onto me for a few years. Then I can learn the rhythm of their seasons:

- Bulbs push their green swan-necked stems up from under last autumn's rot.
- Flower heads whither to wispy seeds which drift, gather, set.
- Leaves pucker, darken, let go of their stems.
- Grasses yellow, lie down, wait for the snow.

*

I'd tried to make a home for us in New Orleans, but I couldn't pay the high cost of bars that stayed open all night for him. By Santa Fe, I'd lost all desire to dig root-deep into that hard clay. He would take the car out in to the emptiest desert, alone, and take handfuls of mushrooms. He said he was trying to find god. God had never been a part of our vows. It was his way of pulling away, too.

*

You can watch a plant grow more easily than you can watch a person grow. A person gets bigger, then older, then smaller—but if you know them well, something about their face always looks the same as it did when you first felt close to them. In the case of plants then, or even cities, perhaps one never knows them so well.

*

My out of town friend—let's call him the guy friend, to differentiate him from my local girlfriend, and because that's what he was—surely complicated things in ways that are difficult to piece together now, my husband having no similar support, no equivalent retort to my need for him, which is surely, in part, what that friend was (there was after all that woman, recall, but she had long moved on herself).

On my guy friend's last night in Santa Fe, we had Indian food and scoped out my new apartment. It was fully furnished, because I was taking little, besides clothes and my books. My husband was angry about the books. Perhaps he was also angry about my friend (don't forget, we stayed one night together in a hotel), but at that time, I couldn't imagine sleeping with someone else ever again (which is to say, nothing happened, nor had I thought it would). Marriage can do that to a certain kind of person, I suspect. I never thought I was that kind of person.

*

At Christmastime, the walkways and window sills all over New Mexico are lined with small brown paper bags each holding some sand and a lit candle. Luminaria, or farolitos, they are called. They are said either to light a path to your home for the Christ child, or to memorialize the dead.

*

By winter, my solitude and my resolve were showing new growth. I would be gone from Santa Fe by February. But on Christmas Day, my first ever alone, I left my small, furnished apartment and walked through the empty streets where a fresh, postcard-perfect snow had fallen, and was falling. A large cross overlooks old town, called the Cross of the Martyrs. I climbed its hill, not thinking at all about martyrs or redemption. It wasn't for the grace of the cross, but for the grace of my own exertion, that I climbed: the curling puffs of my breath before me, the crunch and slip of the ground under my feet.

When I got to the top, I looked down on the snow-stippled pines, the low walls, the glowing arcs of lighted paths, and I picked out the orange window of my apartment, and on the other side of town, the dark mass of trees under which my husband slept. I found the curving road that led to my job. I looked for the lights of my girlfriend's house. I stood there and I sucked the cold, dry air in and I pushed it out. And then I walked back down to the road.

*

We'd left Portland together, in love; we left New Orleans together, too, but troubled. When it came time to leave Santa Fe, we each left on our own. He tried to stay on for awhile after I'd gone, but eventually he returned to the colder mountains he knew as home. We never spoke again. I moved and moved and moved and am still moving. Home for me as a place had eroded; it continues to slip past me as if on some great river.

*

Where I live now, great blankets of snow fall, thicker than in the desert mountains, thicker even than in the Rocky Mountains, where I've also spent some time. The snow here covers everything, softening edges and camouflaging trail hazards. And yet: chickadees and jays scratch out a winter living, and overnight, raccoons leave their pecked footprints across my neighbor's driveway.

I snap on snowshoes, pack some water, and head out into it. I breathe easily in the relative silence and through the work of moving my arms and legs. I keep my own pace with the long-limbed bodies of blackberry and tansy, the bare-limbed trees, the thickly furred winter deer, and always birds, alongside the impressions left by hikers faster and earlier than me. My tracks are almost never the first on the trail, which I find a comfort.

GEOLOGY // an investigation

He said, *Your body is like the Gulf.* And I blushed.

All towns start the same, at the edges where the freeway meets them. The billboards always advertise dentists and divorce lawyers—the bastions of new beginnings; the first buildings are reliably gas stations, fast food drive-thrus, and mobile home parks. Later, the heart of the place opens itself up and it is welcoming or it is not.

He meant,

     of Mexico. It was the largest body of water he'd ever seen. When I strode into it, years before we met, I was stung by jellyfish and bitten by black flies. My body and that Gulf—are you kidding? I never said, later, I hate the Gulf, too. He was trying to be poetic. I was trying to convince myself to stay with him.

Instead, I fled him and his sliding, low-slung deltas. His melting into that shallow, tepid sea, silty ton by ton. I couldn't be a wife again. I disappeared for two weeks into Denali. I wanted to, but couldn't stay there.

*

Alaska is a land of accretion, not dispersion. And I need more, not less. A billion years ago, violent collisions built it acre by acre: a litany of groundscapes became an expanse as micro-continents were shoved into one another by volcanic eruptions and the shifting of tectonic plates. Thrust belts slid from magmatic arcs, and rock bit rock. Archipelagos, mountains, and valleys full of water were left behind. And then, once the collecting had slowed, its stitched patchwork covered the northern half of the globe. It was not cold, then. That came later.

Over coffee she said, *You have geographic solutions to your personal problems,* and laughed lightly.

That whole first year in the desert, a newlywed (digging down through the strata, now, the layers like colored silt and sand), I missed the sea—it was like an acrid taste in the back of my throat, that longing for rhythm. *It's not you, it's me,* I told myself. To him: *I don't even know who I have been here, I'm sorry.* What is the sound the wind makes when it blows through the arms of a saguaro? Which smell stings the nose more, salt or sage? My nightmares regularly featured drowning by sand; I woke coughing.

*

There are probably still two roses blooming like fools on Laurel Street between Napoleon and Tchoupitoulas. I still got homesick, then. The last flowers I planted in the dirt, anywhere, were those roses and some tulips I got for free in the French Quarter. I was trying to make a go of it, lay down real roots. *Right place, right time*, said the woman with the wide straw hat, handing me the bulbs, still damp from the soil in her window box.

I drive through Santa Fe—this time an escape route, rather than a lee. I count the shades of adobe, try to predict the street names and fail. I want to remember the mysticism I imagined a decade ago. Instead, I make a note: *the last time I was here, I was somebody's wife*. When does a change of scenery become a personality disorder? The DSM, mapless, offers no relief.

Maybe I'll move to Anchorage, I thought, scraping yellowed orts off the dishes he'd just washed, before putting them in the cupboards. I wanted to have learned from my mistakes; instead they felt like deer paths I would keep walking again and again to and from the water. I said for a second time, *I will never marry you.* He laughed because it sounded like a joke.

*

He kept the cactus and the lemon tree; I took the mother-in-law's tongue. Even our gardens reflect our secret aggressions, now.

In geology, an *uncomformity* is a missing layer of the Earth's history. It's a lack of proof, a century's worth of centuries blown away, settled under the sea or still floating in a slant of sunlight just this morning, when you woke up late. We know it's gone, because the layers below are jagged, like a mouth propped open. Sometimes, it's difficult to tell the chronological order of the sedimentary deposition: there are many ways for the weather to throw rocks around. There are always parts of the story left out.

Galway Kinnell said, "the killing was just one of those things / difficult to pre-visualize–like a cow, / say, getting hit by lightning."

And over and over I see him on the kitchen floor sobbing about some past lover and me with the words stuck in my mouth for months after, like the skin of a popcorn kernel, *this isn't going to work,*

either.

On the way out of town, the backs of billboards say nothing. From driveway, to side street, to artery, to onramp: departure widens outward as a crack in stone yawns from the point of torsion.

ZUGUNRUHE (MIGRATION) II

Migration is an individual act. Even in a flock of starlings a thousand strong, each bird is deciding for itself whether to stay or go. They take their cues from the opening or closing of certain flowers, and dwindling food supplies, or from the crowd of possible mates slowly thinning, from the way the light lengthens earlier or later each day. Migratory birds are calibrated to a range of seasonal changes informing their bodily restlessness—but even with a mountain of information, the choice is still made, each spring or fall, one bird at a time.

Migrations are dangerous and energy-intensive. A bird must weigh the risk of such a lengthy journey against the risk of starving for food or companionship if they remain. In other words: Migrants would stay in one spot if they could.

*

I lived in seven different homes in Oregon before I left at age 22. With my mother and father in a small white house (I'm told), with my mom in a big brown apartment complex which I remember (we were on the bottom floor), in the house-of-many-interior-colors on Harold when she married and moved in with my stepfather, in the house on Mitchell, then the split level out in Oregon City—a blue collar, conservative suburb. In high school, I briefly lived in a motorhome out in the country, parked in various family members' driveways until we all moved back into the Mitchell street house, and then I had my own two apartments. First, there was the roomy and bright apartment in the Craftsman 4-plex on E Burnside, and then the sagging upstairs apartment on Multnomah, backed up to a buffer of spindly trees next to the freeway, where my husband and I lived just before leaving town for good.

When I think about growing up, I don't think of my family as transient. I always lived on the east side of the river near enough to Portland that it felt like I had a home until I left it. My moving around never felt like a learned response, but an organic one.

*

In the mid '60s Stephen Emlen used a series of specially designed cages to identify how certain songbirds, Indigo buntings specifically (but in test runs of the study two kinds of sparrows, and Dark-eyed juncos, tangentially), navigate during both spring and fall migrations. These birds migrate at night, and Emlen wanted to identify how—in the dark of even moonless nights, and over terrain often changed by human activity—they knew which way to go, year after year.

The cages held one bird each. They had circular bases with short, smooth walls, opening into wide funnels, over which he stretched a ½" garden mesh, so the birds could see the sky, but not escape into it. In the base was an ink pad, and the funnel was lined with blotting paper. As the birds expressed their natural *Zugunruhe*, or migratory restlessness, they would jump up and attempt to fly in the direction they believed they needed to go, and as they did so, their feet would hit the blotting paper, leaving spidery black footprints. Each time they fell back to the bottom of the cage, they were re-inked. Emlen then had data about the direction the birds were hoping to travel.

From the stained blotting paper, Emlen would use a half-page of math to convert the various "attempts" into orderly graphs. He used circles, to approximate a compass, and in each circle, radius lines represented the direction in which the greatest number of hops, or attempts were made, a number noted under and to the left of each

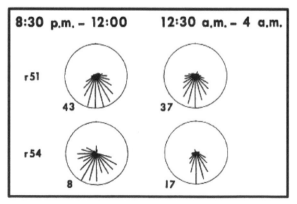

From Emlen 1: "Zuhunruhe orientation under the natural night sky analyzed as a function of time of night; autumn, 1965."

circle. In the first Emlen figure, you can see two charts for two individual birds each, r51 and r54, under natural autumn skies.

Indigo buntings are considered "long distance" migrants, because their migratory route is about 1,200 miles each way. Emlen's buntings were captured near Ann Arbor, Michigan, though they occur as far west as Colorado and Arizona. In 1965, under a natural autumn sky, they would have felt the physical urge, the *Zugunruhe*: a jumpiness, and a fluttering—more than a craving but less than an addiction—to fly toward Florida and the Keys or Central America.

I saw my first Indigo bunting outside of Boulder, Colorado, having driven from Laramie the night before. I was hoping to see a Barn owl hunting in the pre-dawn morning, but only heard one. That same day I saw my first Blue grosbeaks, and at the time, I might have had trouble telling the two apart through the binoculars, but I was in the midst of several experienced birders who had no trouble pointing out distinguishing field marks from 30 yards.

*

Metaphors offer a comfortable distance from which to view many phenomena, a kind of protective shell. For example, if I say that my compulsive fleeing from one place to another, from unassuageable heartache to heartache-to-be, is like a swallow flying year after year, to and from Capistrano, it is so that I can find value in it, instead of shame.

In Europe, white storks have been observed forgoing their annual migration across the Sahara to winter instead in the garbage dumps of Spain and Morocco. Sometimes, the metaphors write themselves.

*

I have amassed a re-collection of interiors, which could also be called homes, for a long time now. All those times I moved, it was not lightly. I had hundreds of boxes. I needed help loading, driving, and unloading, and if I'd been somewhere for too short a time to have made friends who might help, I had to hire hands to do it. It took several people several hours to empty even a studio apartment of mine of my books and seashells and rocks, and pour them into another space. Each time I packed, I would make hard decisions about what I could relinquish (many of those losses, I still lament), and after unpacking, I would begin the slow work of placing everything where it belonged—a distinction established mostly from its spatial relationship to other objects, i.e, some knick knacks belonged on bookshelves, with the books, and others went in windowsills, or on end tables, surrounded by the same objects they were always surrounded by—and then the compulsive work of filling every space left open with new things: espresso cups, running medals, sweaters, feathers, coins from other countries.

In *Collections of Nothing*, William Davies King writes, "If human objects have proven unsteady, material objects might stand in. Collectors resonate unforgettable breakage in the shell of love," in other words, he then quotes Meunsterberger, "such a person requires symbolic substitutes to cope with a world he or she regards as basically unfriendly, even hazardous. So long as he or she can touch and hold and possess and, most importantly, replenish, these surrogates constitute a guarantee of emotional support." Or, without a stable ideation of "home," I carried a house everywhere, reproducing an approximation of comfort.

Even these facts about birds, and when I first saw them from my many different windows and from trains and cars and boats around the world, are a collection started in my grandmother's living room that I can replenish no matter where I land.

Listen: swans have the largest numbers of feathers of all birds—25,000. Hummingbirds, only around a thousand. The longest bird migration on record is that of the Arctic tern: it travels between Greenland and Antarctica each year—a distance of over 44,000 miles. Peregrine falcons are the fastest bird, with aerial dives clocked at over 240 miles per hour.

I once cried harder over the loss of a pink coin bank that *reminded* me of my grandmother than I did over the loss of my grandmother. Because I knew that one day I would lose her.

*

How I moved so much is one conversation. I could tell you about the value of good moving boxes, about the importance of packing them tightly.

Why I moved is a different conversation. At the heart of the answer is a balancing of risks. The risk of wound, of ache, of heartache.

*

I would be remiss if I didn't mention that migratory creatures, birds among us, use many cues, including celestial position, but also dawn and dusk polarization patterns, and information from the Earth's magnetic field, to traverse great distances. Scientists, even after thirty years of research, still don't know how these cues are all integrated, often by birds that migrate effectively without parental intervention. In other words: some birds don't learn so much as know the direction they need to head. And we still don't know how—despite the tiniest electrodes, the most sensitive tracking instruments, the most complex of calculations.

Think about which cues you learned from experience vs those you instinctively understood: the tilt of a cup just before it is dropped as opposed to the solidity of one before it is thrown against a wall to make a point, the rising tone of voice that suggests one should head south or north or west as quickly as possible. Perhaps to aid you in your travels, you, too, have learned to read road maps, train timetables, bus schedules, and subway plans on four different continents.

*

Emlen compiled charts of bird footprints under "natural skies" first, and then he brought the birds into a large planetarium where he could use the dome's mechanism to shift the stars in the sky, to see how the birds would react. He was continuing the work of his father, who strongly believed that nocturnal migrants used the stars to find their way.

Below, you can see how bird g77 responded, when its springtime Zugunruhe was under the dictate of Emlen's swiftly tilting heavens.

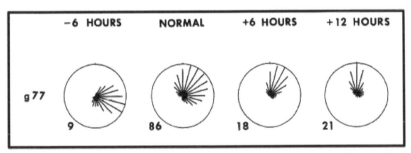

From Emlen 2 "Zugunruhe orientation under temporally shifted skies (± 6 and 12 hours) compared with results obtained under "normal" planetarium conditions (28° N); spring, 1965.""

Turning back the clock caused the most disturbance, perhaps because an earlier night sky signals that snow, instead of the long days of summer, is coming. The radius that slowly points more and more northerly as the sky is shifted later and later into the season looks to me like hurrying. I often see urgency in place of efficiency.

*

Each time I moved in my twenties and early thirties, I would say it was forward: into opportunity. Though it would also be true that men and their anger were at the root of many of my exits. My job disguised the compulsion and fear by offering up out of state transfers just when I could use them. And then, I lost that job, and with it, any hope of "making my life feel 'in progress,'" as Maggie Nelson states in *Bluets,* "rather than a sleeve of ash falling off a lit cigarette." My need to move and move and move was laid bare as a symptom, rather than a cure.

*

Controlling the timing of the stars was not enough to satisfy Emlen's curiosity about the mechanism of the bunting's celestial map. He wanted to know *which* stars mattered most to the birds. He used the planetarium's ability to turn certain stars "off" to narrow down the likely suspects, starting with those used most often by us to navigate the northern hemisphere.

Some birds—and g77 in the third Emlen figure is a solid representative—heeding the springtime urge to head north to their summer haunts could find their way just fine without any of the stars in the southern sky visible, though they made fewer attempts. Fewer still attempts were made with the North Star or the Big Dipper gone, though their sense of direction wasn't grossly impacted. Just their willingness to fly into a sky that must have suddenly looked *wrong*.

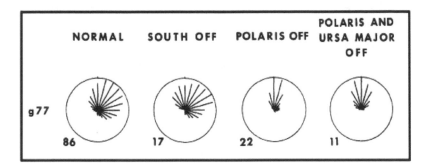

From Emlen 3 "Zugunruhe orientation under partially blocked skies, compared with results obtained under "normal" planetarium conditions (28° N); spring 1965."

In a more recent study on the migration of European cuckoos, eleven of the birds were taken from Norway to Spain, prior to their autumnal migration to Central Africa. Six flew east until they found stopover points that they'd used on previous migrations, and from those points, continued their usual path. Each bird used different points to reconnect to their known route. Five lost their transmitting signal. The birds showed individual decision-making, based on a blend of instincts and experiences.

The first time I heard a Common cuckoo (related to, but different in many ways from our own cuckoos) was in the French Alps.

(That sounds so pompous a thing to say, but it is true: I was once, briefly, a traveler of the world.) I was there looking for vultures, with a Bearded vulture specialist and a tiger keeper, both from Austria.

The sun was rising and the light was slowly creeping between two giant peaks into a wooded valley and I could hear them calling all over. I turned to Hans with unbridled delight and amazement, "They sound just like the clocks!" (Ours sound nothing like the clocks.)

"Of course?" He replied, thinking perhaps that I was dim. Why else would it be called a cuckoo clock, then, was what he was probably thinking.

KUH-koo! KUH-koo! The memory of that moment comes to me like the smell of lilacs or rain in the desert: There is beauty and light and wonder still in the world. Somewhere, maybe even right now in the French Alps, cuckoo birds are chiming the hour.

And somewhere in the Swiss Alps, clockmakers are reproducing the sound in small wooden cabinets, stuffed with clocks-works trailing gold chains, each ending in a cast pinecone.

*

If, for example, I'd sometimes like to imagine that my insecurities are the function of a sublime natural order, a restlessness that speaks to and through stars or tides or tectonic plates, it isn't because I need to feel more important than I am, but less singular.

And if I'd rather think about birds, any bird, really, than all the people I've known who had to choose between relative risks, between an empty or full bed, between an anger that could be predicted and one that could not, it's because I prefer the beauty of feathers and the orderliness of how they lie across a wing in such a way as to permit flight.

*

Canada geese, known for teaching their goslings to migrate in reliable V-formations, are also well-known as both resident and migratory birds. Once nearly extinct in North America, from over-hunting, egg-collecting, and the drying out of wetlands during the end of the 19th-century, Canada geese were beneficiaries of early—and extremely effective—conservation efforts. Our resident birds are descended from those raised in captivity to help restore the species. Even older populations of migrating birds can be enticed to stick around our abundant year-round lawns and municipal ponds.

*

My grandmother died in July, and the following February, my grandfather followed her. My mother said she would have to sell their house, and in an emotional pique, I demanded a chance to buy it.

I'd never lived there, but I was a difficult child, as the family myth goes, and so my mother sent me there often when I was young and unmoved by consequences. What I didn't understand until much later, was that it was at my grandparents' house, that I could be myself: stubborn, messy, and even angry, without risk. I would not be sent away for it, or refused return. I could also be curious and singularly focused one minute and bored the next. And too, their own anger was a predictable response to bad behavior, meted out reasonably, which I would have found a comfort.

When the sale went through, it was more relief than celebration. Coming back hasn't turned me into a different, happier, or less worried person—but I often feel a sense of being where I belong, among familiar objects.

*

The buntings probably surprised Emlen by flying straight without the beacon of the North Star. That fall, he tried again, blotting out vernal stars. In the colder months, losing the Southern sky was more disruptive, as was the loss of Cassiopeia, but not to every bird, every time. His final test was to turn off all the stars. One bird, r58 (not shown), nobly tried twelve times to head generally south, but the rest were struck nearly or completely still by the black, empty heavens.

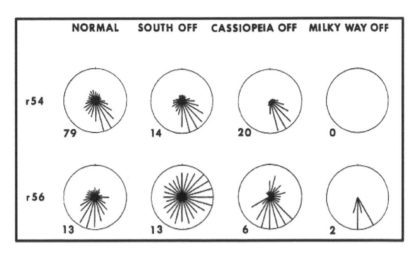

From Emlen 4 "Zugunruhe orientation under partially blocked skies, compared with results obtained under "normal" planetarium conditions (35° N); fall, 1965."

After all his work, Emlen states that one might conclude many things from his diagrams and notes, and many after him have—about which stars in which positions might have the most influence over the buntings—but that ultimately, "in light of the great amount of variation in these data and the small sample size of birds, these interpretations must be considered as highly speculative." Scientific inquiry, like the mess of living it seeks to inform, can resist our inclinations to order its results.

*

In Oregon, the Anna's hummingbird stays through the winter, though all other hummingbirds flee for warmer weather. What I am trying to say is: if you must, go, but if you can, stay.

*

There are birds on every continent. Right now, there are birds near you—in the trees, or on the ground, looking for something you've dropped, or lined up on the wires, or in the sky overhead, barreling toward something.

*

The fate of the thirty-three buntings from Emlen's experiments is not recorded in the literature.

Acknowledgements

Many thanks first and foremost to Jesi Buell of KERNPUNKT Press for believing in this manuscript and being such a thoughtful and supportive editor.

Thank you to everyone who read the book in part or in whole before anyone else, especially Kati, Silas, Erica, Lauren, Rebecca, and Irina.

Books are not made alone. Many people helped me, both financially and emotionally, during this process. I will not be able to list them all, as it would take another book to do so. Please accept the inadequacy and incompleteness of this list, and my apologies for any omissions. Thank you to Marvin, for everything. Thank you to my mom, and the rest of my family, for all the ways you've supported me and my creative life. Thank you to Rachel, Nichole, Mandy, Birgit, Stephanie, Kate and Ericka, Katie, Sara, Juniper and Kelly for your generous hearts. Thank you to everyone who bought one of my chapbooks or let me crash at your place or gave me a ride. Thank you to my thesis committee, Andy, Frieda, Mark, and the rest of the faculty at University of Wyoming's MFA and thank you to my cohort, for helping to nurture several of these essays from infancy to publication. Thank you to Jennifer and Peter at Colgate for giving me a year to write as the O'Connor fellow, and thank you to Javier for being the best fellow-fellow I could hope for. Thank you to the amazing writers I met while at Ucross, who inspired me to keeping trying. Thank you to the fine people at Hedgebrook for the time and space that made some of this work possible. And thank you to the kind folks at Breadloaf and Fine Arts Work Center for connecting me with fantastic mentors who inspired some of these essays, especially Jane and Joanne.

Thank you to the editors who first championed and published many of these essays. Critical Learning Period first appeared in *New Ohio Review*. Safari Club first appeared in *52/250: A Year of Flash*. Kick Ball Change first appeared in *River Teeth*'s "Beautiful Things." How to Skin a Bird first appeared in *Shenandoah*. Crazy first appeared in *Sweet Lit*. Brown Rat,

American Crow, and Domestic Cat first appeared in *Brevity*. Dragonfly, Rainbow Trout, Box Turtle, and Borer Beetle first appeared in *The Fiddleback*. Horned Lark, Red-winged Blackbird, and House Sparrow first appeared in *The Fourth River*. The Dogs first appeared in *Anthropoid*. Phrenology first appeared in *Hayden's Ferry Review*. Notes on Arrival first appeared in *New Mexico Review*. An earlier version of Meteorology appeared in *Wilder Quarterly*. An earlier version of Bone appeared in *Flyway*. Pyrology first appeared in *Sonora Review*. Notes Toward a Partial Definition of Home first appeared in *Waveform: Twenty-first Century Essays by Women* (University of Georgia Press, 2016), edited by Marcia Aldrich. Geology first appeared in *Passages North*. Thank you for Sal and Kevin at Etchings Press/University of Indianapolis for publishing my chapbooks and giving me hope that I might be able to find homes and readers for my work.

Chelsea Biondolillo is the author of two prose chapbooks, *Ologies* and *#Lovesong*. Her work has been collected in *Best American Science and Nature Writing 2016, Waveform: Twenty-first Century Essays by Women,* and *How We Speak To One Another: An Essay Daily Reader,* among others. She is a former Olive B. O'Connor fellow at Colgate University, and her work has been supported by Literary Arts, Wyoming Arts Council and the Consortium for Science and Policy Outcomes/NSF. She has a BFA in photography from Pacific NW College of Art and an MFA in creative writing/environmental studies from the University of Wyoming. She lives and works outside of Portland, Oregon.

Photographer: Kerry McQuaid